THE COOK'S
POTATO BOOK

PRACTICAL HANDBOOK

THE COOK'S
POTATO BOOK

SALLY MANSFIELD

LORENZ BOOKS

This edition published by Lorenz Books

© Anness Publishing Limited 2000

Lorenz Books is an imprint of
Anness Publishing Limited
Hermes House
88-89 Blackfriars Road
London SE1 8HA

www.lorenzbooks.com

This edition distributed in Canada by, Raincoast Books
8680 Cambie Street, Vancouver, British Columbia V6P 6M9

A CIP catalogue record for this book is available from the British Library

Publisher: Joanna Lorenz
Executive Editor: Linda Fraser
Editor: Rebecca Clunes
Indexer: Hilary Bird
Editorial Reader: Diane Ashmore
Production Controller: Yolande Denny
Designer: Margaret Sadler
Photography: Steve Moss (potatoes) and Sam Stowell (recipes)
Food for Photography: Alex Barker (techniques), Eliza Baird (recipes)
Additional Recipes: Roz Denny, Jacks Clarke, Joanna Farrow, Shirley Gill, Sarah Gates,
Steven Wheeler, Hilaire Walden, Christine France, Rosamund Grant, Sheila Kimberley, Liz Trigg,
Carla Capalbo, Carole Clements, Judy Jackson, Ruby Le Bois, Chris Ingram, Matthew Drennan,
Elizabeth Wolfe-Cohen, Shehzad Hussain, Rafi Fernandez, Manisha Kanini, Laura Washburn,
Andi Clevely, Katherine Richmond, Jennie Shapter

Also published as *More than Mash* and, as part of a larger compendium, *Potato*

1 3 5 7 9 10 8 6 4 2

Notes
For all recipes, quantities are given in both metric and imperial measures and, where appropriate,
measures are also given in standard cups and spoons. Follow one set, but not a mixture because
they are not interchangeable.

Standard spoon and cup measures are level.
1 tsp = 5ml, 1 tbsp = 15ml, 1 cup = 250ml/8fl oz

Australian standard teaspoons are 20ml. Australian readers should
use 3 tsp in place of 1 tbsp for measuring small quantities of gelatine, cornflour, salt etc.

Medium potatoes and eggs are used unless otherwise stated.

CONTENTS

INTRODUCTION

Now that there is such a huge variety of potatoes to choose from, suited to every kind of cooking, it is important to think about how you plan to use them before going shopping. Being tempted by some creamy International Kidneys or lovely little Pink Fir Apple potatoes, when what you want to make is a velvety thick soup, will not result in complete success. Many supermarkets and pre-packed potatoes provide an indication of cooking techniques suitable for the particular variety. If you always like to eat the skins and are concerned about what may have been sprayed on them, you would be well advised to buy organic potatoes. Alternatively, grow your own – a very easy and rewarding task providing you have the space.

BUYING

All potatoes should be firm. Avoid any which are soft, flabby, sprouting or have a white dusty mould. Check for any green patches. These are a sign that the potatoes have been stored in the light and, although the rest of the potato is fine to eat, you do need to cut out these poisonous patches. Do not buy any potatoes that have extensive green patches on the skin.

When buying new potatoes, check that they are really young and fresh by scraping the skin, which should peel off easily. New potatoes have a high vitamin C content, so buy and eat them as fresh as possible.

STORING

Potatoes grow in the dark and like to stay in the dark; they do not keep well unless they are properly stored. In the

warmth of a centrally heated kitchen they can start sprouting; the dampness of a cold fridge will make them sweaty and mouldy, and stored in too much light, they begin to lose their nutritional value and start to turn green. Unless potatoes can be kept in a cool, dark frost-free place, such as a larder or garage, it is better to buy them in small quantities, so that they are used quickly. The ideal temperature to store potatoes is 7–10°C/45–50°F.

When you buy potatoes in a plastic bag, remove them from it immediately when you get home, then store them in a suitable place. If you are storing your potatoes in the house, place them in an open storage rack in a dry, dark place, or in a paper bag or hessian sack. Potatoes should not be cleaned with water before you store them as they may start to go mouldy.

Read the advice on storage on pre-packed potatoes, as these come in many varieties. Some are ready to cook and others are already peeled or cleaned. You can even buy potatoes with seasonings or flavoured butter, but these are best consumed soon after purchase – read the packet for correct storage times.

PREPARATION TECHNIQUES

The method used to prepare potatoes affects their nutritional content. Much of the goodness and flavour is in the skin and just under it so keep the skins on when you can. Vitamin C can be lost whilst the potatoes are soaking in water before and during the cooking process. It is best not to prepare potatoes much in advance of cooking.

Cleaning Potatoes

Nowadays, most potatoes, especially those from supermarkets and pre-packed potatoes, are very clean, so giving them a light wash just before use will probably be sufficient. Locally grown, farm shop or home-grown potatoes may still have some earth attached to them, so give them a light scrub before cooking, using a small scrubbing brush or a gentle scourer if necessary. With new potatoes this will probably remove the peel as well. Examine the potato for any black eyes and discoloured patches and remove with a potato peeler or pointed knife.

Peeling Potatoes

You can boil potatoes and peel them afterwards as soon as they are cool. This is much easier and gives a fresher and earthier taste. If you need to peel them while they are still hot for immediate eating or because you are in a hurry, hold the hot potato with a fork and gently peel off the skin.

To peel potatoes before cooking, use a very sharp potato peeler to remove the thinnest layer of skin possible in long even strips. Place the potatoes in a saucepan of water so that they are just covered until ready to cook, but preferably cook them immediately to avoid any loss of vitamin C.

Scraping Potatoes

Really new potatoes peel very easily. Often, all that is required is to rub them in your hands.

Otherwise, use a small sharp knife to scrape away the flaky skin and place in just enough water to cover.

CUTTING POTATOES

Both the size and shape of the pieces into which potatoes are cut will affect the cooking technique.

Chopping

Potatoes are often chopped for recipes such as salads and dishes using leftovers. If you are cooking them first, use a waxy variety which will stay firm. They chop most easily when they are cold and peeled. Cut the potato in half, then in half again and again, until it is evenly cut to the size required.

Dicing

Dicing requires greater precision to produce even-shaped cubes.

1 First, trim the potato into a neat rectangle (keep the trimmings for soup), then cut into thick even slices.

2 Stack the slices, turn the stack over and cut into thick batons and, finally, into even cubes the required size.

Grating

Depending on their use, potatoes can be grated before or after cooking. After cooking is easier, but avoid overcooking, especially if they are floury, or they will just fall to pieces. When the potatoes are cool, grate on a large blade straight into the cooking dish or frying pan.

Raw potatoes exude a lot of starchy liquid when grated. Check before you start whether this is required for the recipe. If the liquid is not required, grate raw potatoes on a board using a standard grater. If the liquid is required, grate into a medium bowl, using either the medium or large blade. Squeeze the liquid from the potatoes by hand. Don't grate raw potatoes too soon as the flesh quickly begins to turn brown.

Slicing

It may not always matter how evenly you slice potatoes, but it can affect both the appearance and the cooking time of some dishes. Always use a large, sharp knife. Cut across the width of the potato for rounder slices and along the length for longer slices. Put the tip of the knife on the board first, then press the heel of the knife down firmly to create even slices. For most casseroles and toppings, cut slices 3mm/⅛in thick. If you need to slice cooked potatoes for a recipe, undercook them slightly and let them cool completely first.

Crisps

You can make small quantities of thick crisps by hand. Hold one end of the potato firmly in your hand and cut thin slices with a sharp knife on a chopping board. To make thinner crisps by hand, use the slicing blade on a standard grater or a mandoline.

Hold the grater firmly on a chopping board, placing a damp cloth on the board to anchor the grater. Carefully slide the potato down over the slicing blade. Make sure the blade is very sharp and adjust it to the right thickness. If it is not adjustable, you will find that the harder you press, the thicker the crisps will be.

Follow the manufacturer's instructions for using a mandoline. Use the handle or gadget that is provided with some versions whenever possible. Use the fluted blade for crinkle-cut crisps. Take particular care when the potato gets smaller, as it is easy to cut the fingers. For "waffled" crisps – *pommes gaufrettes* – cut horizontally down the blade, rotating each time you slice to get a lattice effect.

If you want to make a large batch of plain-shaped crisps, slice the potatoes in a food processor.

Ribbons

Thin ribbons, which also deep-fry into delicious crisps, can simply be cut with a potato peeler. Peel the potato flesh round and round as if peeling an apple. Work quickly or put the ribbons in a bowl of cold water as you go to prevent them from turning brown. (Any leftover odd shapes can go in the stock pot.)

Chips

The larger you cut chips, the healthier they will be, since they will absorb less fat during cooking. You can also make chips with their skins on, providing additional fibre.

For traditional English chips, use the largest chipping potatoes. Cut them into 1.5cm/⅝in thick slices, or thicker if you wish. Turn the slices on their sides and cut into 1.5cm/⅝in batons.

Chips can be cut with a special chip cutter and some mandolines. Cut the potatoes to a suitable size to fit.

For a healthier alternative, cut chips, extra thick, into wedge shapes. First cut the potatoes in half lengthways, then into long thin wedges.

For potato matchsticks – *pommes allumettes* – cut the potato into a neat rectangle, then thin slices and, finally, julienne strips about 3mm/⅛in thick.

COOKING TECHNIQUES

There are endless different ways of cooking potatoes. The best technique depends on both the potato variety and the dish you are cooking.

Blanching

Potatoes may be blanched to soften the skin for easy peeling, to remove excess starch or to parcook before roasting. Use a draining spoon to remove large pieces, but place smaller pieces in a chip basket for easy removal.

Place the potatoes in a pan of cold water. Bring to the boil over a low heat and simmer for 2–5 minutes, depending on their size. Drain and use or leave in the cooling water until required.

Boiling

This is the simplest way of cooking potatoes. They may be cooked whole or in chunks, but should be evenly sized. They can be boiled with or without skins; to retain the colour of sweet potatoes cook them in their skins. Floury potatoes need very gentle boiling or the outside will cook before the inside is ready. New potatoes should be put straight into boiling water and cooked for about 15 minutes, but maincrop potatoes should be put into cold water and brought gradually to the boil. Very firm salad potatoes can be put into boiling water, simmered for 5–10 minutes, then left to stand in the hot water for a further 10 minutes.

1 Place the potatoes in a large pan, add just enough water to cover and 5–10ml/ 1–2 tsp salt. Bring to the boil over a low heat and boil gently for 15–20 minutes.

2 When they are cooked, drain the potatoes in a colander, then return them to the pan to dry off. For really dry, peeled potatoes – for mashing, for example – place them over a very low heat to drive off all the moisture.

Steaming

All potatoes steam well, but this method is ideal for floury varieties and those which fall apart easily. New potatoes are also delicious steamed in their skins.

1 Place the prepared potatoes in a sieve, colander or steamer over a deep pan of boiling water. You can place a handful of mint leaves in the steamer first, if liked. Cover tightly and steam for 5–7 minutes if sliced small and up to 20 minutes if large.

2 Test with a sharp knife towards the end of the cooking time, turn off the heat and leave until required.

Shallow-frying

The key to success is using a good fat. A mixture of butter and olive oil gives a good flavour, yet allows a higher cooking temperature than butter alone. Use a large heavy-based pan for even cooking and to allow room for turning.

1 Heat about 25g/1oz/2 tbsp butter and 30ml/2 tbsp oil in a large, heavy based frying pan until bubbling. Add an even layer of cooked or parcooked potatoes. Leave for 4–5 minutes, until the undersides turn golden.

2 Turn the potatoes over gently with a large fish slice once or twice during cooking until golden brown all over.

Deep-frying

Fry in small batches so that the temperature does not drop too much when you add the potatoes. Remove any burnt pieces after each batch.

1 Dry the chips on kitchen paper. Half fill a deep, heavy-based saucepan or a deep-fat fryer with clean fat. Heat to 190°C/375°F or until a cube of bread turns golden in 1 minute.

2 Heat the basket in the fat, then add the chips to it and gradually lower into the pan. Cook, shaking the basket occasionally, until they are golden and crisp. Remove with a draining spoon or chip basket and drain well against the side of the pan. Tip the chips on to kitchen paper to drain excess fat.

Microwaved Potatoes

Baking in a microwave is a great time saver, but does not produce the delicious crunchy crust of oven-baked potatoes.

1 Prick the skins of new potatoes or potato pieces. Place large potatoes in a circle on kitchen paper on the microwave tray and make cuts around the middle so the skins don't burst.

2 Allow 4–6 minutes on high, adding 2–4 minutes for every additional potato. Turn once during cooking.

To boil, place small potatoes in a microwave bowl with 30–45ml/2–3 tbsp water. Cover tightly with microwave film, pierce two or three times and cook for 10–12 minutes per 450g/1lb on high. Leave to stand for 3–5 minutes before draining and serving.

Cooking in a Clay Pot

This is most like cooking in a bonfire or under a pile of earth – but here the potatoes take on a deep woody aroma and intense flavour without all the charring and smoke. The terracotta pot takes a generous 450g/1lb potatoes. Soak the pot in water for 10–20 minutes before using.

1 Put small, even-size potatoes, preferably in their skins, in the pot. Toss in 30–45ml/2–3 tbsp olive oil or melted butter and sprinkle with salt and ground black pepper. Add any flavourings, such as a garlic clove, herbs or bacon.

2 Cover the pot and place in a cold oven. Allow to heat to 200°C/400°F/ Gas 6. After 40–45 minutes, test with the point of a knife. When tender, serve straight from the pot.

Baking

Allow a 275–350g/10–12oz potato for a good size portion and choose a variety recommended for baking. Sprinkle ordinary potatoes with salt and sweet potatoes with a little demerara sugar.

1 Wash and dry the potatoes, then rub with oil and sprinkle with salt. Place on a baking sheet and cook in a hot oven at 220°C/425°F/Gas 7 for 1–1½ hours for large potatoes or 40–60 minutes for medium. To speed up the cooking time and ensure even cooking, cook the potatoes on a skewer or a special potato baking rack.

2 To test that the potatoes are cooked, squeeze the sides gently. Cut a cross in the top of each one and set aside to cool slightly. Hold the potato in a clean cloth and squeeze gently to open up. Serve with a pat of butter in each. Other simple toppings include grated cheese or soured cream and chopped herbs.

Baked Potato Skins

Bake the potatoes as above, then cut in half and scoop out the soft centres. (Mash and reserve for a supper or pie topping.) Brush the skins with melted butter, margarine or a mixture of butter and oil and return to the oven for 20 minutes, or until crisp and golden.

Potato Parcels

Baking in a foil or greaseproof paper parcel makes for a tasty potato with no mess or dirty dishes.

Wash or scrub and dry small potatoes, then wrap them up in a greaseproof paper or foil parcel with several knobs of butter, a sprinkling of seasoning and a sprig or two of mint, tarragon or chives. Bake in a preheated oven at 190°C/375°F/Gas 5 for 40–50 minutes for 450g/1lb potatoes.

Roasting

For soft, fluffy-centred roast potatoes, use large baking potatoes – Wilja, Maris Piper, Record, Désirée and Kerr's Pink all give excellent results. The choice of fat and the temperature are critical. Beef dripping gives the best results and goose fat, if you are lucky enough to find some, produces light, crisp potatoes. Otherwise, use lard, dripping from the joint, light olive oil or a mixture of sunflower and olive oils. Use a large roasting tin, so there is room to turn the potatoes, and make sure it is hot.

1 Blanch peeled chunks of potato in boiling water for 5 minutes, then leave in the cooling water for 5 minutes. Drain and return to the pan to dry off. Either shake the pan or fork over the surfaces of the potatoes to roughen them.

2 Pour a shallow layer of fat into a heavy roasting tin and heat in the oven at 220°C/425°F/Gas 7. Add the potatoes and toss in the hot oil. Return the tin to the oven and roast for up to 1 hour. Once or twice, remove the tin from the oven and turn the potatoes over, using a spatula. Then drain off any excess fat so they can crisp and brown.

Mashing

The humble mashed potato has seen a revival in recent years, but you've got to start with good mash. Sweet potatoes and floury potatoes are good choices, producing a light, fluffy mash, while waxy potatoes will result in a dense and rather gluey purée. Boil even-size potatoes until very well cooked but not falling apart and dry them well, as watery potatoes will give a soggy, heavy mixture. Cold potatoes mash best of all.

You can mash potatoes in several ways. A hand masher, with a strong but open cutting grid, gives a smooth yet textured result; pressing the potatoes through a ricer or sieve gives a light, fluffy mash; a fork can result in a slightly lumpy, uneven texture. An electric hand-held mixer can be used but don't use a food processor as it will not give good results.

For a low-calorie side dish, simply mash the potatoesl. Alternatively beat in a generous knob of butter, some creamy milk and seasoning, then continue mashing until you have a fluffy mixture.

Soups, Starters and Finger Food

Nothing beats a hot bowl of soup, and the flavour combinations are endless, from a clam and mushroom chowder to a spicy chorizo soup. For a smart dinner party, try Coquilles St Jacques with its decorative piped border. Potatoes also make a simple, tasty snack; they are a good choice as finger food at a buffet.

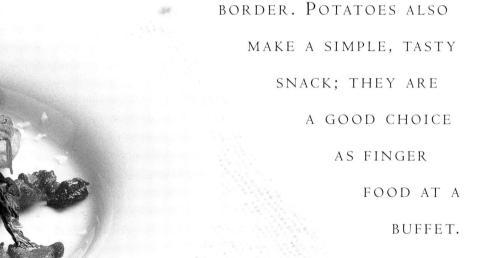

LEEK AND POTATO SOUP

THESE TWO VEGETABLES MAKE A REALLY TASTY AND SUBSTANTIAL, SIMPLE SOUP, AND ARE READILY
AVAILABLE THROUGHOUT THE YEAR, MAKING THEM IDEAL FOR ANY SEASON.

SERVES FOUR

INGREDIENTS
50g/2oz/4 tbsp butter
2 leeks, chopped
1 small onion, finely chopped
350g/12oz floury potatoes, chopped
900ml/1½ pints/3¾ cups chicken or
  vegetable stock
salt and ground black pepper
crusty bread, to serve

1 Heat 25g/1oz/2 tbsp of the butter in a large heavy-based saucepan, add the chopped leeks and onion and cook gently, stirring occasionally so that they do not stick to the bottom of the pan, for about 7 minutes until softened but not browned.

2 Add the potatoes to the pan and cook, stirring occasionally, for 2–3 minutes. Add the stock and bring to the boil then reduce the heat, cover and simmer gently for 30–35 minutes until the vegetables are very tender.

3 Season to taste, remove the pan from the heat and stir in the remaining butter in small pieces. Serve hot with slices of thick crusty bread.

COOK'S TIP
If you prefer your soup to have a smoother consistency, simply press the mixture through a sieve or pass through a food mill once it is cooked. Don't use a food processor as it can give the potatoes a gluey texture.

CLAM, MUSHROOM AND POTATO CHOWDER

THE DELICATE, SWEET SHELLFISH TASTE OF CLAMS AND THE SOFT EARTHINESS OF WILD MUSHROOMS
COMBINE WITH POTATOES TO MAKE THIS A GREAT MEAL ON ITS OWN — FIT FOR ANY OCCASION.

SERVES FOUR

INGREDIENTS
48 clams, scrubbed
50g/2oz/4 tbsp unsalted butter
1 large onion, chopped
1 celery stick, sliced
1 carrot, sliced
225g/8oz assorted wild mushrooms,
  such as chanterelles, saffron milk-
  caps, chicken of the woods or
  St George's mushrooms, sliced
225g/8oz floury potatoes,
  thickly sliced
1.2 litres/2 pints/5 cups light
  chicken or vegetable stock, boiling
1 thyme sprig
4 parsley stalks
salt and ground black pepper
thyme sprigs, to garnish

1 Place the clams in a large saucepan, discarding any that are open. Put 1cm/½in of water in the pan, cover, bring to the boil and steam over a medium heat for 6–8 minutes until the clams open (discard any clams that do not open).

2 Drain the clams over a bowl, remove the shells from each one and chop. Strain the cooking juices into the bowl, add the chopped clams and set aside.

3 Add the butter, onion, celery and carrot to the pan and cook gently until softened but not coloured. Add the mushrooms and cook for 3–4 minutes until their juices begin to appear. Add the potatoes, the clams and their juices, the stock, thyme and parsley stalks.

4 Bring to the boil then reduce the heat, cover and simmer for 25 minutes. Season to taste, ladle into soup bowls, and garnish with thyme.

CREAMED SPINACH AND POTATO SOUP

THIS IS A DELICIOUS LOW-FAT CREAMY SOUP. THIS RECIPE USES SPINACH BUT OTHER VEGETABLES WOULD WORK JUST AS WELL, SUCH AS CABBAGE OR SWISS CHARD.

SERVES FOUR

INGREDIENTS
  1 large onion, finely chopped
  1 garlic clove, crushed
  900g/2lb floury potatoes, diced
  2 celery sticks, chopped
  1.2 litres/2 pints/5 cups
    vegetable stock
  250g/9oz fresh spinach leaves
  200g/7oz/scant 1 cup low-fat
    cream cheese
  300ml/½ pint/1¼ cups milk
  dash of dry sherry
  salt and ground black pepper
  chopped fresh parsley, to garnish
  crusty bread, to serve

1 Place the onion, garlic, potatoes, celery and stock in a large saucepan. Simmer for 20 minutes.

2 Season the soup and add the spinach, cook for a further 10 minutes. Remove from the heat and cool slightly.

3 Process the soup in batches in a food processor or food mill and return to the saucepan.

4 Stir in the cream cheese and milk, simmer and check for seasoning. Add a dash of sherry and serve crusty bread and chopped fresh parsley.

POTATO AND GARLIC BROTH

ALTHOUGH THERE IS PLENTY OF GARLIC IN THIS SOUP, THE END RESULT IS NOT OVERPOWERING. SERVE PIPING HOT WITH BREAD, AS THE PERFECT WINTER WARMER.

SERVES FOUR

INGREDIENTS
  2 small or 1 large whole head of
    garlic (about 20 cloves)
  4 medium potatoes, diced
  1.75 litres/3 pints/7½ cups
    vegetable stock
  salt and ground black pepper
  flat leaf parsley, to garnish

VARIATION
Make the soup more substantial by placing in each bowl a slice of French bread which has been toasted and topped with melted cheese. Pour the soup over so that the bread soaks it up.

1 Preheat the oven to 190°C/375°F/ Gas 5. Place the unpeeled garlic bulbs or bulb in a small roasting tin and bake for 30 minutes until they are soft in the centre.

2 Meanwhile, par-boil the potatoes in a large saucepan of lightly salted boiling water for 10 minutes.

3 Simmer the stock for 5 minutes. Drain the potatoes and add to the stock.

4 Squeeze the garlic pulp into the soup, reserving a few cloves to garnish, stir and season to taste. Simmer for 15 minutes and serve garnished with whole cloves and parsley.

KALE, CHORIZO AND POTATO SOUP

THIS HEARTY WINTER SOUP HAS A SPICY KICK TO IT, WHICH COMES FROM THE CHORIZO SAUSAGE. THE SOUP BECOMES MORE POTENT IF CHILLED OVERNIGHT AND IT IS WORTH BUYING THE BEST POSSIBLE CHORIZO SAUSAGE TO IMPROVE THE FLAVOUR.

SERVES SIX TO EIGHT

INGREDIENTS
   225g/8oz kale, stems removed
   225g/8oz chorizo sausage
   675g/1½lb red potatoes
   1.75 litres/3 pints/7½ cups
      vegetable stock
   5ml/1 tsp ground black pepper
   pinch cayenne pepper (optional)
   12 slices French bread, grilled
   salt and ground black pepper

1 Place the kale in a food processor and process for a few seconds to chop it finely.

2 Prick the sausages and place in a pan with enough water to cover. Simmer for 15 minutes. Drain and cut into thin slices.

3 Boil the potatoes for about 15 minutes or until tender. Drain, and place in a bowl, then mash adding a little of the cooking liquid to form a thick paste.

4 Bring the vegetable stock to the boil and add the kale. Add the chorizo and simmer for 5 minutes. Add the paste gradually, simmer for 20 minutes. Season with black pepper and cayenne.

5 Place bread slices in each bowl, and pour the soup over. Serve sprinkled with pepper.

SMOKED HADDOCK AND POTATO SOUP

"CULLEN SKINK" IS A CLASSIC SCOTTISH DISH USING ONE OF THE COUNTRY'S TASTIEST FISH.
THE RESULT IS A THICK, CREAMY SOUP WITH A RICH, SMOKY FISH FLAVOUR.

SERVES SIX

INGREDIENTS

350g/12oz smoked haddock fillet
1 onion, chopped
bouquet garni
900ml/1½ pints/3¾ cups water
500g/1¼lb floury potatoes, quartered
600ml/1 pint/2½ cups milk
40g/1½oz/3 tbsp butter
salt and ground black pepper
snipped chives, to garnish
crusty bread, to serve

1 Put the haddock, onion, bouquet garni and water into a large heavy-based saucepan and bring to the boil. Skim the scum from the surface, then cover, reduce the heat and poach gently for 10–15 minutes until the haddock flakes easily.

2 Lift the haddock from the pan and cool slightly, then remove the skin and bones. Flake the flesh and put to one side. Return the skin and bones to the pan and simmer, for 30 minutes.

3 Strain the fish stock and return to the pan, then add the potatoes and simmer for about 25 minutes. Remove the potatoes from the pan. Add the milk to the pan and bring to the boil.

4 Mash the potatoes with the butter, then whisk into the soup. Add the flaked fish to the pan and heat through. Season. Ladle into soup bowls, sprinkle with chives and serve with crusty bread.

CORN AND SWEET POTATO SOUP

*THE COMBINATION OF SWEETCORN AND SWEET POTATO GIVES THIS SOUP A REAL DEPTH OF FLAVOUR
AS WELL AS MAKING IT LOOK VERY COLOURFUL.*

SERVES SIX

INGREDIENTS
  15ml/1 tbsp olive oil
  1 onion, finely chopped
  2 garlic cloves, crushed
  1 small red chilli, seeded and
    finely chopped
  1.75 litres/3 pints/7½ cups
    vegetable stock
  10ml/2 tsp ground cumin
  1 medium sweet potato, diced
  ½ red pepper, finely chopped
  450g/1lb sweetcorn kernels
  salt and ground black pepper
  lime wedges, to serve

1 Heat the oil and fry the onion for 5 minutes until softened. Add the garlic and chilli and fry for a further 2 minutes.

2 In the same pan, add 300ml/½ pint/ 1¼ cups of the stock, and simmer for 10 minutes.

3 Mix the cumin with a little stock to form a paste and then stir into the soup. Add the diced sweet potato, stir and simmer for 10 minutes. Season and stir again.

4 Add the pepper, sweetcorn and remaining stock and simmer for 10 minutes. Process half of the soup until smooth and then stir into the chunky soup. Season and serve with lime wedges for squeezing over.

MINESTRONE GENOA

*THE VARIATIONS ON THIS SOUP ARE ENDLESS. THIS PASTA-FREE VERSION IS PACKED WITH HEAPS
OF VEGETABLES TO MAKE A SUBSTANTIAL, HEARTY LUNCH WITH CRUSTY BREAD.*

SERVES SIX

INGREDIENTS
  1.75 litres/3 pints/7½ cups
    vegetable stock
  1 large onion, chopped
  3 celery sticks, chopped
  2 carrots, finely diced
  2 large floury potatoes, finely diced
  ½ head of cabbage, very finely diced
  225g/8oz runner beans, sliced
    diagonally
  2 x 400g/14oz cans cannellini
    beans, drained
  60ml/4 tbsp ready-made pesto sauce
  salt and ground black pepper
  crusty bread, to serve
  freshly grated Parmesan cheese,
    to serve

1 Pour the stock into a large saucepan. Add the onion, celery and carrots. Simmer for 10 minutes.

2 Add the potatoes, cabbage, and beans and simmer for 10–12 minutes or until the potatoes are tender.

3 Stir in the cannellini beans and pesto, and bring the mixture to the boil. Season to taste and serve hot with crusty bread and plenty of freshly grated Parmesan cheese.

CATALAN POTATO BROAD BEAN SOUP

BROAD BEANS ARE ALSO KNOWN AS FAVA BEANS. WHILE THEY ARE IN SEASON FRESH BEANS ARE
PERFECT, BUT TINNED OR FROZEN WILL MAKE AN IDEAL SUBSTITUTE.

SERVES SIX

INGREDIENTS
  30ml/2 tbsp olive oil
  2 onions, chopped
  3 large floury potatoes, diced
  450g/1lb fresh broad beans
  1.75 litres/3 pints/7½ cups
    vegetable stock
  1 bunch coriander, finely chopped
  150ml/¼ pint/⅔ cup single cream
  salt and ground black pepper
  coriander leaves, to garnish

COOK'S TIP
Broad beans sometimes have a tough
outer skin, particularly if they are large.
To remove this, first cook the beans
briefly, peel off the skin, and add the
tender centre part to the soup.

1 Heat the oil in a large saucepan
and fry the onions, stirring occasionally,
for about 5 minutes until softened but
not brown.

2 Add the potatoes, beans (reserving a
few for garnishing) and stock to the
mixture in the saucepan and bring to
the boil, then simmer for 5 minutes.

3 Stir in the coriander and simmer for
a further 10 minutes.

4 Process in batches in a blender or
food processor, then return the soup to
the pan.

5 Stir in the cream (reserving a little for
garnishing), season, and bring to a
simmer. Serve garnished with more
coriander leaves, beans and cream.

SPANISH POTATO AND GARLIC SOUP

SERVED IN EARTHENWARE DISHES, THIS CLASSIC SPANISH SOUP SHOULD BE SAVOURED.

SERVES SIX

INGREDIENTS
  30ml/2 tbsp olive oil
  1 large onion, finely sliced
  4 garlic cloves, crushed
  1 large potato, halved and cut into
    thin slices
  5ml/1 tsp paprika
  400g/14oz can chopped
    tomatoes, drained
  5ml/1 tsp thyme leaves
  900ml/1½ pints/3¾ cups
    vegetable stock
  5ml/1 tsp cornflour
  salt and ground black pepper
  chopped thyme leaves, to garnish

1 Heat the oil in a large saucepan,
fry the onions, garlic, potato and
paprika for 5 minutes, until the onions
have softened, but not browned.

2 Add the tomatoes, thyme and stock
and simmer for 15–20 minutes until the
potatoes have cooked through.

3 Mix the cornflour with a little water to
form a paste and stir into the soup, then
simmer for 5 minutes until thickened.

4 Using a wooden spoon break the
potatoes up slightly. Season to taste.
Serve garnished with the chopped
thyme leaves.

LEEK, POTATO AND ROCKET SOUP

ROCKET ADDS ITS DISTINCTIVE, PEPPERY TASTE TO THIS WONDERFULLY SATISFYING SOUP.
SERVE IT HOT, GARNISHED WITH A GENEROUS SPRINKLING OF TASTY CIABATTA CROÛTONS.

SERVES FOUR TO SIX

INGREDIENTS
  50g/2oz/4 tbsp butter
  1 onion, chopped
  3 leeks, chopped
  2 medium floury potatoes, diced
  900ml/1½ pints/3¾ cups light
    chicken stock or water
  2 large handfuls rocket, roughly
    chopped
  150ml/¼ pint/⅔ cup double cream
  salt and ground black pepper
  garlic-flavoured ciabatta croûtons,
    to serve

1 Melt the butter in a large heavy-based pan then add the onion, leeks and potatoes and stir until the vegetables are coated in butter. Heat the ingredients until sizzling then reduce the heat to low.

2 Cover and sweat the vegetables for 15 minutes. Pour in the stock or water and bring to the boil then reduce the heat, cover again and simmer for 20 minutes until the vegetables are tender.

3 Press the soup through a sieve or pass through a food mill and return to the rinsed-out pan. (When puréeing the soup, don't use a blender or food processor, as these will give the soup a gluey texture.) Add the chopped rocket to the pan and cook the soup gently, uncovered, for 5 minutes.

4 Stir in the cream, then season to taste and reheat gently. Ladle the soup into warmed soup bowls and serve with a scattering of garlic-flavoured ciabatta croûtons in each.

SAVOURY POTATO CAKES

GOLDEN AND CRISP, BUT SOFT WHEN YOU BITE INTO THEM, THESE POTATO CAKES ARE A TASTY APPETIZER. THEY CAN ALSO BE SERVED FOR BREAKFAST OR SUPPER, WITH OR WITHOUT ANYTHING ELSE.

SERVES FOUR

INGREDIENTS

450g/1lb waxy potatoes
1 small onion, grated
4 slices streaky bacon, finely
  chopped
30ml/2 tbsp self-raising flour
2 eggs, beaten
vegetable oil, for deep-frying
salt and ground black pepper
parsley, to garnish

VARIATION
For a vegetarian alternative, omit the
bacon and replace it with red pepper.

1 Coarsely grate the potatoes, rinse,
drain and pat dry on kitchen paper,
then mix with the onion, half the bacon,
flour, eggs and seasoning.

2 Heat a 1cm/½in layer of oil in a
frying pan until really hot, then add
about 15ml/1 tbsp of the potato mixture
and quickly spread the mixture out with
the back of the spoon taking care that it
does not break up.

3 Add a few more spoonfuls of the
mixture in the same way, leaving space
between each one so they do not stick
together, and fry them for 4–5 minutes
until golden on the undersides.

4 Turn the cakes over and fry the other
side. Drain on kitchen paper, transfer to
an ovenproof dish and keep warm in a
low oven while frying the remainder. Fry
the remaining bacon and parsley and
serve sprinkled over the hot cakes.

COQUILLES ST JACQUES

A CLASSIC FRENCH STARTER, THAT CALLS FOR THE BEST QUALITY SCALLOPS POSSIBLE TO ENSURE A TRULY WONDERFUL RESULT. YOU WILL NEED FOUR SCALLOP SHELLS TO SERVE THESE.

SERVES FOUR

INGREDIENTS
   450g/1lb potatoes, chopped
   50g/2oz/4 tbsp butter
   4 large or 8 small scallops
   120ml/4fl oz/½ cup fish stock
For the sauce
   25g/1oz/2 tbsp butter
   25g/1oz/¼ cup plain flour
   300ml/½ pint/1¼ cups milk
   30ml/2 tbsp single cream
   115g/4oz/1 cup mature Cheddar
      cheese, grated
   salt and ground black pepper
   dill sprigs, to garnish
   grilled lemon wedges, to serve

1 Preheat oven to 200°C/400°F/Gas 6. Place the chopped potatoes in a large saucepan, cover with water and boil for 15 minutes or until tender. Drain and mash with the butter.

2 Spoon the mixture into a piping bag fitted with a star nozzle. Pipe the potatoes around the outside of a cleaned scallop shell. Repeat the process, making four in total.

3 Simmer the scallops in a little fish stock for 3 minutes or until just firm. Drain and slice the scallops finely. Set them aside.

4 To make the sauce, melt the butter in a small saucepan, add the flour and cook over a low heat for a couple of minutes, gradually add the milk and cream, stirring continuously and cook until thickened.

5 Stir in the cheese and cook until melted. Season to taste. Spoon a little sauce in the base of each shell. Divide the scallops between the shells and then pour the remaining sauce over the scallops.

6 Bake the scallops for 10 minutes or until golden. Garnish with dill. Serve with grilled lemon wedges.

TWICE BAKED GRUYÈRE AND POTATO SOUFFLÉ

A GREAT STARTER DISH, THIS RECIPE CAN BE PREPARED IN ADVANCE IF YOU ARE ENTERTAINING AND GIVEN ITS SECOND BAKING JUST BEFORE YOU SERVE IT UP.

2 Stir in half of the Gruyère cheese and all of the flour. Season to taste with salt and pepper.

3 Finely chop the spinach and fold into the potato mixture.

4 Whip the egg whites until they form soft peaks. Fold a little of the egg white into the mixture to loosen it slightly. Using a large spoon, fold the remaining egg white into the mixture.

5 Grease 4 large ramekin dishes. Pour the mixture in and place on a baking sheet and bake for 20 minutes. Remove from the oven and allow to cool.

6 Turn the soufflés out on to a baking sheet and scatter with the remaining cheese. Bake again for 5 minutes and serve with salad leaves.

SERVES FOUR

INGREDIENTS
  225g/8oz floury potatoes
  2 eggs, separated
  175g/6oz/1½ cups Gruyère, grated
  50g/2oz/½ cup self-raising flour
  50g/2oz spinach leaves
  butter for greasing
  salt and ground black pepper
  salad leaves, to serve

VARIATION
For a different flavouring try replacing the Gruyère with a crumbled blue cheese, such as Stilton or Shropshire Blue, which have a stronger taste to them.

1 Preheat the oven to 200°C/400°F/ Gas 6. Cook the potatoes in lightly salted boiling water for 20 minutes until very tender. Drain and mash with the 2 egg yolks.

NEW POTATOES WITH MOCK CAVIAR AND CREAM CHEESE

A PERFECT ONE-BITE SNACK FOR A PARTY THAT MAKES THE MOST OF TENDER NEW POTATOES WITH THEIR WAXY TEXTURE. DANISH MOCK CAVIAR IS ANOTHER NAME FOR LUMPFISH ROE.

MAKES THIRTY

INGREDIENTS
    30 small new potatoes
    200g/7oz/scant 1 cup full-fat
        cream cheese
    15ml/1 tbsp chopped fresh parsley
    1 jar Danish black mock caviar
        (lumpfish roe)
    1 jar salmon roe
    salt and ground black pepper
    dill sprigs, to garnish

VARIATION
If you can't get hold of any mock caviar, then top the new potatoes with thin slices of smoked salmon.

1 Cook the potatoes in a large saucepan of boiling water for 20 minutes or until tender. Drain through a colander and then trim off both ends of each potato.

2 Sit the potatoes on the cut end. Beat the cream cheese and parsley together and season. Spoon the mixture on to the potatoes and top with a little mock caviar and salmon roe. Garnish with dill.

POTATO BLINIS

THIS CRISP, LIGHT PANCAKE ORIGINATES FROM RUSSIA, WHERE IT IS SERVED WITH THE BEST CAVIAR, OR USE THE TOPPING FROM THE RECIPE ABOVE, IF YOU PREFER.

SERVES SIX

INGREDIENTS
    115g/4oz maincrop potatoes, boiled
        and mashed
    15ml/1 tbsp easy-blend dried yeast
    175g/6oz/1½ cups plain flour
    oil for greasing
    90ml/6 tbsp soured cream
    6 slices smoked salmon
    salt and ground black pepper
    lemon slices, to garnish

COOK'S TIP
These small pancakes can easily be prepared in advance and stored in the refrigerator until ready for use. Simply warm them up in a low oven.

1 In a large bowl, mix together the potatoes, yeast, flour and 300ml/½ pint/1¼ cups hand-hot water.

2 Leave to rise in a warm place for 30 minutes until the mixture has doubled in size.

3 Heat a non-stick frying pan and add a little oil. Drop spoonfuls of the mixture on to the preheated pan. Cook the blinis for 2 minutes until lightly golden on the underside, toss with a spatula and cook on the second side. Season to taste before serving.

4 Serve with a little soured cream and a small slice of smoked salmon folded on top. Garnish with black pepper and a small slice of lemon.

DEEP-FRIED NEW POTATOES
WITH SAFFRON AÏOLI

SERVE THESE CRISPY LITTLE GOLDEN POTATOES DIPPED INTO A WICKEDLY GARLICKY MAYONNAISE —
THEN WATCH THEM DISAPPEAR IN A MATTER OF MINUTES!

SERVES FOUR

INGREDIENTS
1 egg yolk
2.5ml/½ tsp Dijon mustard
300ml/½ pint/1¼ cups extra virgin
olive oil
15–30ml/1–2 tbsp lemon juice
1 garlic clove, crushed
2.5ml/½ tsp saffron strands
20 baby, new or salad potatoes
vegetable oil, for deep frying
salt and ground black pepper

1 For the aïoli, put the egg yolk in a bowl with the mustard and a pinch of salt. Mix. Beat in the olive oil very slowly, drop by drop, then in a thin stream. Add the lemon juice.

2 Season the aïoli with salt and pepper then add the crushed garlic and beat the mixture thoroughly to combine.

3 Place the saffron in a small bowl and add 10ml/2 tsp hot water. Press the saffron with the back of a teaspoon, to extract the colour and flavour, and leave to infuse for 5 minutes. Beat the saffron and the liquid into the aïoli.

4 Cook the potatoes in their skins in boiling salted water for 5 minutes, then turn off the heat. Cover the pan and leave for 15 minutes. Drain the potatoes, then dry them thoroughly in a tea towel.

5 Heat a 1cm/½in layer of vegetable oil in a deep pan. When the oil is very hot, add the potatoes and fry quickly, turning, until crisp and golden. Drain on kitchen paper and serve hot with the saffron aïoli.

MINI BAKED POTATOES WITH BLUE CHEESE

PERFECT AS FINGER FOOD FOR A PARTY, ESPECIALLY AS YOU CAN PREPARE THEM IN ADVANCE.

MAKES TWENTY

INGREDIENTS
  20 small new or salad potatoes
  60ml/4 tbsp vegetable oil
  coarse salt
  120ml/4fl oz/½ cup soured cream
  25g/1oz blue cheese, crumbled
  30ml/2 tbsp chopped fresh chives,
    for sprinkling

COOK'S TIP
This dish works just as well as a light
snack; if you don't want to be bothered
with lots of fiddly small potatoes, simply
bake an ordinary baking potato.

1 Preheat the oven to 180ºC/350ºF/
Gas 4. Wash and dry the potatoes. Pour
the oil into a bowl. Add the potatoes
and toss to coat well with oil.

2 Dip the potatoes in the coarse salt to
coat lightly. Spread out the potatoes on
a baking sheet. Bake for 45–50 minutes
until tender.

3 In a small bowl, combine the soured
cream and blue cheese.

4 Cut a cross in the top of each potato.
Press gently with your fingers to open
the potatoes.

5 Top each potato with a dollop of the
cheese mixture. It will melt down into
the potato nicely. Sprinkle with chives
on a serving dish and serve hot or at
room temperature.

SWEET POTATO CRISPS

YOU CAN USE THESE PINK POTATOES TO MAKE SWEET OR SAVOURY CRISPS, AND THEY HAVE A LOVELY COLOUR AND A UNIQUE, ALMOST FRUITY FLAVOUR.

SERVES FOUR

INGREDIENTS
   2 medium sweet potatoes
   vegetable oil, for deep-frying
   salt

VARIATIONS
For a sweet version, sprinkle with cinnamon and caster sugar, and toss well, before cooling. You can prepare yams in just the same way.

COOK'S TIP
These sweet potato crisps are delicious served warm, but if you don't manage to finish them they are equally good as a cold snack. Serve with a dip, either sweet or savoury.

1 Peel the sweet potatoes under cold running water, cut into 3mm/⅛in thick slices with a sharp knife or vegetable slicer and place in a bowl of salted cold water.

2 Heat a 1cm/½in layer of oil in a large saucepan or deep-fat fryer. While the oil is heating, remove the slices from the water and pat dry on kitchen paper.

3 Fry a few slices at a time until crisp, then drain on kitchen paper. Sprinkle with salt and serve warm.

INDIAN POTATO PANCAKES

ALTHOUGH CALLED A PANCAKE, THESE CRISPY SPICED CAKES ARE MORE LIKE A BHAJI. THEY MAKE AN IDEAL STARTER FOR A MEAL WITH A CURRY AS THE MAIN DISH.

MAKES TEN

INGREDIENTS
   300g/11oz potatoes, grated
   25ml/1½ tsp garam masala or curry
      powder
   4 spring onions, finely chopped
   1 large egg white, lightly beaten
   30ml/2 tbsp vegetable oil
   salt and ground black pepper
   chutney and relishes, to serve

COOK'S TIP
Don't grate the potatoes too soon before use as the flesh will quickly turn brown.

1 Using your hands, squeeze the excess liquid from the grated potatoes and pat dry.

2 Place the dry, grated potatoes in a separate bowl and add the spices, spring onions, egg white and seasoning, stir to combine.

3 Heat a non-stick frying pan over a medium heat and add the oil.

4 Drop tablespoonfuls of the potato on to the pan and flatten out with the back of a spoon (you will need to cook the pancakes in two batches).

5 Cook for a few minutes and then flip the pancakes over. Cook for a further 3 minutes.

6 Drain on kitchen paper and serve with chutney and relishes.

MIDDLE EASTERN LAMB AND POTATO CAKES

AN UNUSUAL VARIATION, THESE MINCED LAMB TRIANGLES ARE EASY TO SERVE HOT FOR A BUFFET, OR THEY CAN BE EATEN COLD AS A SNACK OR FOR PICNICS.

MAKES TWELVE TO FIFTEEN

INGREDIENTS
  450g/1lb new or small, firm potatoes
  3 eggs
  1 onion, grated
  30ml/2 tbsp chopped fresh parsley
  450g/1lb finely minced lean lamb
  115g/4oz/2 cups breadcrumbs
  vegetable oil, for frying
  salt and ground black pepper
  mint leaves, to garnish
  pitta bread and herby green salad,
    to serve

1 Cook the potatoes in a large pan of boiling salted water for 20 minutes until tender, then drain and leave to cool. Beat the eggs in a large bowl. Add the onion, parsley and seasoning and beat together.

2 When the potatoes are cold, grate them coarsely and stir into the egg mixture together with the minced lamb. Knead for 3–4 minutes until all the ingredients are thoroughly blended.

3 Take a handful of the lamb mixture and roll it into a ball. Repeat this process until all is used. Roll the balls in the breadcrumbs and then mould them into triangular shapes, about 13cm/5in long. Coat them in the breadcrumbs again on both sides.

4 Heat a 1cm/½in layer of oil in a frying pan over a medium heat. When the oil is hot, fry the potato cakes for 8–12 minutes until golden brown on both sides, turning occasionally. Drain on kitchen paper. Serve hot, garnished with mint and accompanied by pitta bread and salad.

IDAHO POTATO SLICES

THIS SUBSTANTIAL STARTER IS MADE FROM A LAYERED RING OF POTATOES, CHEESE AND HERBS.
COOKING THE INGREDIENTS TOGETHER GIVES THEM A VERY RICH FLAVOUR.

3 Scatter some of the onion rings over the potatoes and top with a little of the cheese. Scatter over some thyme and then continue to layer the ingredients, finishing with cheese and seasoning.

4 Press the potato layers right down. (The mixture may seem quite high at this point but it will cook down.)

5 Pour the cream over and cook in the oven for 35–45 minutes. Remove from the oven and cool. Invert on to a plate and cut into wedges. Serve with a few salad leaves.

VARIATION
If you want to make this dish more substantial, top the wedges with slices of grilled bacon, or grilled red peppers.

SERVES FOUR

INGREDIENTS
  3 large potatoes
  butter, for greasing
  1 small onion, finely sliced into rings
  200g/7oz/1¾ cups red Leicester or
    mature Cheddar cheese, grated
  fresh thyme sprigs
  150ml/¼ pint/⅔ cup single cream
  salt and ground black pepper
  salad leaves, to serve

1 Preheat the oven to 200°C/400°F/ Gas 6. Peel the potatoes and cook in boiling water for 10 minutes until they are just starting to soften. Remove from the water and pat dry.

2 Finely slice the potatoes, using the straight edge of a grater or a mandoline. Grease the base and sides of an 18cm/ 7in cake tin with butter and lay some of the potatoes on the base to cover it completely. Season.

Salads and Side Dishes

WARM OR CHILLED POTATOES ADD A NEW DIMENSION TO SALADS. ADD FLAVOUR AND COLOUR TO CHUNKY CUT POTATOES WITH SLICED RADISHES, OR TRY A PIQUANT CARIBBEAN SALAD. CLASSIC POTATO SIDE DISHES HAVE LONG BEEN ESSENTIAL PARTNERS TO NUMEROUS MAIN COURSES. TRY SOMETHING A LITTLE DIFFERENT TO SERVE ALONGSIDE A SIMPLE ROAST, SUCH AS BOULANGÈRE POTATOES OR OVEN CHIP ROASTIES. AND ADD A GARLIC TWIST TO MASH — PERFECT ON ITS OWN OR TO GO WITH A MAIN COURSE.

THE SIMPLEST POTATO SALAD

THE SECRET OF THIS POTATO SALAD IS TO MIX THE POTATOES WITH THE DRESSING WHILE THEY ARE STILL HOT SO THAT THEY ABSORB IT. THIS IS PERFECT WITH GRILLED PORK, LAMB CHOPS OR ROAST CHICKEN OR FOR VEGETARIANS SERVE WITH A SELECTION OF ROASTED VEGETABLES.

SERVES FOUR TO SIX

INGREDIENTS
675g/1½lb small new or
  salad potatoes
4 spring onions
45ml/3 tbsp olive oil
15ml/1 tbsp white wine vinegar
175ml/6fl oz/¾ cup good
  mayonnaise, preferably home-made
45ml/3 tbsp snipped chives
salt and ground black pepper

1 Cook the potatoes in their skins in a large saucepan of boiling salted water until tender.

2 Meanwhile, finely chop the white parts of the spring onions along with a little of the green parts; they look more attractive cut on the diagonal. Put to one side.

3 Whisk together the oil and vinegar. Drain the potatoes well and place them in a large bowl, then immediately toss lightly with the vinegar mixture and spring onions. Put the bowl to one side to cool.

4 Stir the mayonnaise and chives into the potatoes, season well and chill thoroughly until ready to serve. Adjust the seasoning before serving.

POTATO AND RADISH SALAD

RADISHES ADD A SPLASH OF CRUNCH AND PEPPERY FLAVOUR TO THIS HONEY-SCENTED SALAD. SO MANY POTATO SALADS ARE DRESSED IN A THICK SAUCE. THIS ONE HOWEVER, IS QUITE LIGHT AND COLOURFUL WITH A TASTY YET DELICATE DRESSING.

SERVES FOUR TO SIX

INGREDIENTS
450g/1lb new or salad potatoes
45ml/3 tbsp olive oil
15ml/1 tbsp walnut or hazelnut oil
  (optional)
30ml/2 tbsp wine vinegar
10ml/2 tsp coarse-grain mustard
5ml/1 tsp honey
about 6–8 radishes, thinly sliced
30ml/2 tbsp snipped chives
salt and ground black pepper

VARIATIONS
Sliced celery, diced red onion and/or chopped walnuts would make good alternatives to the radishes if you can't get hold of any.

COOK'S TIP
For best effect, serve on a platter lined with frilly lettuce leaves.

1 Cook the potatoes in their skins in a large saucepan of boiling salted water until just tender. Drain the potatoes through a colander and leave to cool slightly. When cool enough to handle, cut the potatoes in half, but leave any small ones whole. Return the potatoes to a large bowl.

2 To make the dressing, place the oils, vinegar, mustard, honey and seasoning in a bowl. Mix them together until thoroughly combined.

3 Toss the dressing into the potatoes in the bowl while they are still cooling and leave to stand for an hour or so to allow the flavours to penetrate.

4 Finally mix in the sliced radishes and snipped chives and chill in the fridge until ready to serve.

5 When ready to serve, toss the salad mixture together again, as some of the dressing may have settled on the bottom and adjust the seasoning.

CURRIED POTATO SALAD
WITH MANGO DRESSING

THIS SWEET AND SPICY SALAD IS A WONDERFUL ACCOMPANIMENT TO ROASTED MEATS.

SERVES FOUR TO SIX

INGREDIENTS
15ml/1 tbsp olive oil
1 onion, sliced into rings
1 garlic clove, crushed
5ml/1 tsp ground cumin
5ml/1 tsp ground coriander
1 mango, peeled, stoned and diced
30ml/2 tbsp demerara sugar
30ml/2 tbsp lime juice
900g/2lb new potatoes, cut in half
   and boiled
15ml/1 tbsp sesame seeds
salt and ground black pepper
deep fried coriander leaves,
   to garnish

1 Heat the oil in a frying pan and fry the onion and garlic over a low heat for 10 minutes until they start to brown.

2 Stir in the cumin and coriander and fry for a few seconds. Stir in the mango and sugar and fry for 5 minutes, until soft. Remove the pan from the heat and squeeze in the lime juice. Season with salt and pepper to taste.

3 Place the potatoes in a large bowl and spoon the mango dressing over. Sprinkle with sesame seeds and serve whilst the dressing is still warm. Garnish with the coriander leaves.

POTATO SALAD WITH CAPERS
AND BLACK OLIVES

A DISH FROM SOUTHERN ITALY, THE COMBINATION OF OLIVES, CAPERS AND ANCHOVIES IS PERFECT.

SERVES FOUR TO SIX

INGREDIENTS
900g/2lb large white potatoes
50ml/2fl oz/¼ cup white wine vinegar
75ml/5 tbsp olive oil
30ml/2 tbsp chopped flat leaf parsley
30ml/2 tbsp capers, finely chopped
50g/2oz/½ cup pitted black olives,
   chopped in half
3 garlic cloves, finely chopped
50g/2oz marinated anchovies
   (unsalted)
salt and ground black pepper

VARIATION
If you want to serve this dish to vegetarians, simply omit the anchovies, it tastes delicious even without them.

1 Boil the potatoes in their skins in a large pan for 20 minutes or until just tender. Remove from the pan using a slotted spoon and place them in a separate bowl.

2 When the potatoes are cool enough to handle, peel off the skins.

3 Cut the peeled potatoes into even chunks and place in a large, flat earthenware dish.

4 Mix together the vinegar and oil, season to taste and add the parsley, capers, olives and garlic. Toss carefully to combine and then pour over the potato chunks.

5 Lay the anchovies on top of the salad. Cover with a cloth and leave the salad to settle for 30 minutes or so before serving to allow the flavours to penetrate.

WARM POTATO SALAD WITH HERB DRESSING

Toss the potatoes in the dressing as soon as possible, so the flavours are fully absorbed. Use the best olive oil for an authentic Mediterranean taste.

SERVES SIX

INGREDIENTS

   1kg/2¼lb waxy or salad potatoes
   90ml/6 tbsp extra virgin olive oil
   juice of 1 lemon
   1 garlic clove, very finely chopped
   30ml/2 tbsp chopped fresh herbs
     such as parsley, basil or thyme
   salt and ground black pepper
   basil leaves, to garnish

1 Cook the potatoes in their skins in boiling salted water, or steam them until tender.

2 Meanwhile make the dressing. Mix together the olive oil, lemon juice, garlic, herbs and season the mixture thoroughly.

3 Drain the potatoes and leave to cool slightly. When they are cool enough to handle, peel them. Cut the potatoes into chunks and place in a large bowl.

4 Pour the dressing over the potatoes while they are still warm and mix well. Serve at once, garnished with basil leaves and black pepper.

WARM HAZELNUT AND PISTACHIO SALAD

Two kinds of crunchy nuts turn ordinary potato salad into a really special accompaniment. It would be lovely with cold sliced roast beef, tongue or ham, but you can serve it on its own as a healthy snack.

SERVES FOUR

INGREDIENTS

   900g/2lb small new or salad potatoes
   30ml/2 tbsp hazelnut or walnut oil
   60ml/4 tbsp sunflower oil
   juice of 1 lemon
   25g/1oz/¼ cup hazelnuts
   15 pistachio nuts
   salt and ground black pepper
   flat leaf parsley sprig, to garnish

VARIATION
Use chopped walnuts in place of the hazelnuts. Buy the broken pieces of nut, which are less expensive than walnut halves, but chop them smaller before adding to the salad.

1 Cook the potatoes in their skins in boiling salted water for about 10–15 minutes until tender.

2 Drain the potatoes well and leave to cool slightly.

3 Meanwhile mix together the hazelnut or walnut oil with the sunflower oil and lemon juice. Season well.

4 Using a sharp knife, roughly chop the nuts.

5 Put the cooled potatoes into a large bowl and pour the dressing over. Toss to combine.

6 Sprinkle the salad with the chopped nuts. Serve immediately, garnished with flat leaf parsley.

NEW POTATO AND QUAIL'S EGG SALAD

FRESHLY COOKED EGGS AND TENDER POTATOES MIX PERFECTLY WITH THE FLAVOUR OF CELERY SALT AND THE PEPPERY TASTING ROCKET LEAVES.

SERVES SIX

INGREDIENTS
900g/2lb new potatoes
50g/2oz/4 tbsp butter
15ml/1 tbsp snipped chives
a pinch of celery salt
a pinch of paprika
12 quail's eggs
a few rocket leaves
salt and ground black pepper
snipped chives, to garnish

COOK'S TIP
You can buy bags of rocket, on its own, or mixed with other leaves, in many supermarkets. It is also easy to grow from seed and makes a worthwhile addition to a herb patch.

1 Boil the potatoes in a large saucepan of salted water for 20 minutes or until tender. Meanwhile, beat the butter and chives together with the celery salt and the paprika.

2 Whilst the potatoes are cooking, boil the eggs for 3 minutes, drain and plunge into cold water. Peel the eggs under running water.

3 Arrange the rocket leaves on plates and divide the eggs between. Drain the potatoes and add the seasoned butter. Toss well to melt the butter and spoon the potatoes on to the plates. Garnish the salad with a few more chives.

BEETROOT AND POTATO SALAD

A BRIGHTLY COLOURED SALAD WITH A LOVELY TEXTURE. THE SWEETNESS OF THE BEETROOT CONTRASTS PERFECTLY WITH THE TANGY DRESSING.

SERVES FOUR

INGREDIENTS
4 medium beetroot
4 potatoes, peeled and diced
1 red-skinned onion, finely chopped
150ml/¼ pint/⅔ cup low-fat yogurt
10ml/2 tsp cider vinegar
2 small sweet and sour cucumbers,
   finely chopped
10ml/2 tsp creamed horseradish
salt and ground black pepper
parsley sprigs, to garnish

COOK'S TIP
To save yourself time and energy, buy ready cooked and peeled beetroot. They are readily available in most supermarkets.

1 Boil the beetroot in a large saucepan, in plenty of water for 40 minutes or until tender.

2 Meanwhile, boil the potatoes in a separate saucepan for 20 minutes until just tender.

3 When the beetroot are cooked, rinse and pull the skins off, chop into rough pieces and place in a bowl. Drain the potatoes and add to the bowl with the onions. Mix the yogurt, vinegar, cucumbers and horseradish. Reserve a little for a garnish and pour the remainder over the salad. Toss and serve with parsley sprigs and dressing.

MARINATED BEEF AND POTATO SALAD

THIS DISH NEEDS TO MARINATE OVERNIGHT, BUT ONCE YOU HAVE DONE THAT IT IS VERY QUICK TO ASSEMBLE AND MAKES A SUBSTANTIAL MAIN MEAL.

SERVES SIX

INGREDIENTS
    900g/2lb sirloin steak
    3 large white potatoes
    ½ red pepper, seeded and diced
    ½ green pepper, seeded and diced
    1 small red skinned onion,
        finely chopped
    2 garlic cloves, crushed
    4 spring onions, diagonally sliced
    1 small cos lettuce, leaves torn
    salt and ground black pepper
    olive oil, to serve
    Parmesan cheese shavings, to serve
For the marinade
    120ml/4fl oz/½ cup olive oil
    120ml/4fl oz/½ cup red wine vinegar
    90ml/6 tbsp soy sauce

1 Place the beef in a large, non-metallic container. Mix together the marinade ingredients. Season with pepper and pour over the meat.

2 Cover and leave to marinate for several hours, or overnight.

3 To prepare the salad, drain the marinade from the meat and pat the joint dry. Preheat the frying pan, cut the meat carefully into thin slices and fry for a few minutes until just cooked on each side, but still slightly pink. Set aside to cool.

4 Using a melon baller, scoop out rounds from each potato. Boil in lightly salted water for 5 minutes or until just tender.

5 Drain and transfer to a bowl, and add the remaining ingredients. Transfer to a plate with the beef. Drizzle with a little extra olive oil and serve with Parmesan.

CARIBBEAN POTATO SALAD

COLOURFUL VEGETABLES IN A CREAMY SMOOTH DRESSING MAKE THIS PIQUANT SALAD IDEAL TO SERVE ON ITS OWN OR WITH GRILLED OR COLD MEATS.

SERVES SIX

INGREDIENTS

900g/2lb small waxy or
  salad potatoes
2 red peppers, seeded and diced
2 celery sticks, finely chopped
1 shallot, finely chopped
2 or 3 spring onions, finely chopped
1 mild fresh green chilli, seeded and
  finely chopped
1 garlic clove, crushed
10ml/2 tsp finely snipped chives
10ml/2 tsp finely chopped basil
15ml/1 tbsp finely chopped parsley
15ml/1 tbsp single cream
30ml/2 tbsp salad cream
15ml/1 tbsp mayonnaise
5ml/1 tsp Dijon mustard
7.5ml/½ tbsp sugar
snipped chives, to garnish
chopped red chilli, to garnish

1 Cook the potatoes in a large saucepan of boiling water until tender but still firm. Drain and leave to one side. When cool enough to handle, cut into 2.5cm/1in cubes and place in a large salad bowl.

2 Add all the vegetables to the potatoes in the salad bowl, together with the chilli, garlic and all the chopped herbs.

3 Mix together the cream, salad cream, mayonnaise, mustard and sugar in a small bowl. Stir well until the mixture is thoroughly combined and forms a smooth dressing.

4 Pour the dressing over the potato mixture and stir gently to coat evenly. Serve garnished with the snipped chives, and chopped red chilli.

ITALIAN SALAD

A COMBINATION OF ANTIPASTO INGREDIENTS AND POTATOES MAKES THIS A VERY SUBSTANTIAL DISH.

SERVES SIX

INGREDIENTS
    1 aubergine, sliced
    75ml/5 tbsp olive oil
    2 garlic cloves, cut into slivers
    4 sun-dried tomatoes in oil, halved
    2 red peppers, halved, seeded and
      cut into large chunks
    2 large baking potatoes, cut
      into wedges
    10ml/2 tsp mixed dried Italian herbs
    30–45ml/2–3 tbsp balsamic vinegar
    salt and ground black pepper

1 Preheat the oven to 200°C/400°F/
Gas 6. Place the aubergines in a
medium roasting tin with the olive oil,
garlic and sun-dried tomatoes. Lay the
pepper chunks over the aubergines.

2 Lay the potato wedges on top of the
other ingredients in the roasting tin.
Scatter the herbs over and season with
salt and black pepper. Cover the tin
with foil and bake in the oven for
45 minutes.

3 Remove from the oven and turn the
vegetables over. Then return to the oven
and cook uncovered for 30 minutes.
Remove the vegetables with a slotted
spoon. Add the vinegar and seasoning
to the pan, whisk and pour over the
vegetables. Season with salt and
black pepper.

PINK FIR APPLE POTATO SALAD

A RICH MUSTARD SAUCE GIVES THE POTATOES ADDED FLAVOUR AND COLOUR.

SERVES FOUR TO SIX

INGREDIENTS
    5 eggs
    30–45ml/2–3 tbsp Dijon mustard
    200g/7oz jar mayonnaise
    3 celery sticks, finely chopped
    115g/4oz bacon lardons
    900g/2lb Pink Fir Apple potatoes
    30ml/2 tbsp chopped flat leaf parsley
    salt and ground black pepper

1 Place the eggs carefully into a saucepan of water and bring to the boil. Simmer for 5–8 minutes, drain and plunge the eggs straight into a bowl containing cold water.

2 Peel the eggs and mash three of them in a large bowl with a fork. Stir in the mustard, mayonnaise, celery and seasoning. Thin down with a little water if you wish. Set aside.

3 Dry fry the bacon until crisp and toss half of it into the mayonnaise mixture. Reserve the remainder.

4 Boil the potatoes for 20 minutes until tender. Drain and leave to cool. Toss into the mayonnaise mixture and spoon into a serving platter. Slice the remaining eggs and scatter over the salad with the reserved bacon pieces. Scatter the parsley over the top and serve.

MARQUIS POTATOES

A VARIATION ON THE DUCHESSE MIXTURE, FINISHED WITH A DELICIOUSLY TANGY TOMATO MIXTURE SET IN THE CENTRE OF THE POTATO NEST.

SERVES SIX

INGREDIENTS
   900g/2 lb floury potatoes
   450g/1lb ripe tomatoes
   15ml/1tbsp olive oil
   2 shallots, finely chopped
   25g/1oz/2 tbsp butter
   3 egg yolks
   60ml/4 tbsp milk
   chopped fresh parsley, to garnish
   sea salt and ground black pepper

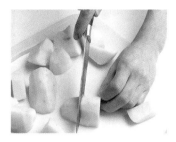

1 Peel and cut the potatoes into small chunks, boil in lightly salted water for 20 minutes or until very tender. Meanwhile, blanch the tomatoes in boiling water and then plunge into a bowl of cold water. Peel the skins and then scoop the seeds out. Chop the tomato flesh.

2 Heat the olive oil in a large frying pan and fry the shallots for 2 minutes stirring continuously. Add the chopped tomatoes to the pan and fry for a further 10 minutes until the moisture has evaporated. Set aside.

3 Drain the potatoes through a colander and return to the pan and allow the steam to dry off. Cool slightly and mash well with the butter and 2 of the egg yolks and the milk. Season with salt and ground black pepper.

4 Grease a baking sheet. Spoon the potato into a piping bag fitted with a medium star nozzle. Pipe six oval nests onto the baking sheet. Beat the remaining egg with a little water and carefully brush over the potato. Grill for 5 minutes or until golden.

5 Spoon the tomato mixture inside the nests and top with a little parsley. Serve them immediately.

POTATO PIZZA

THIS "PIZZA" MADE OF MASHED POTATOES, WITH A ROBUSTLY FLAVOURED FILLING OF ANCHOVIES,
CAPERS AND TOMATOES, IS A SPECIALITY OF PUGLIA IN NORTHERN ITALY.

SERVES FOUR

INGREDIENTS

1kg/2¼lb floury potatoes
120ml/4fl oz/½ cup extra virgin
  olive oil
2 garlic cloves, finely chopped
350g/12oz tomatoes, chopped
3 anchovy fillets, chopped
30ml/2 tbsp capers, rinsed
salt and ground black pepper

1 Cook the potatoes in their skins in boiling water until tender. Drain well and leave to cool slightly. When they are cool enough to handle, peel and mash or pass through a food mill. Beat in 45ml/3 tbsp of the oil and season to taste. Set aside.

2 Heat another 45ml/3 tbsp of the oil in a medium saucepan. Add the garlic and the chopped tomatoes and cook over a medium heat for 12–15 minutes stirring a little to cook evenly, until the tomatoes soften and begin to dry out. Meanwhile preheat the oven to 200°C/400°F/Gas 6.

3 Oil a round shallow baking dish. Spread half the mashed potatoes into the dish in an even layer. Cover with the tomatoes, and dot with the chopped anchovies and the capers.

4 Spread over the rest of the potatoes in an even layer. Brush the top with the remaining oil and bake for 20–25 minutes until the top is golden brown. Sprinkle with black pepper and serve hot.

VARIATION

For a vegetarian version of this dish, simply omit the anchovies. A few pitted and chopped olives may be added to the filling instead. Add them in step 3, on top of the tomatoes.

BYRON POTATOES

A MEAL IN ITSELF, THIS DISH IS BASED ON BAKED POTATOES WITH A RICH CREAMY CHEESE FILLING.

SERVES SIX

INGREDIENTS
   3 baking potatoes
   115g/4oz/1 cup mature Cheddar
   cheese, grated
   90ml/6 tbsp single cream
   sea salt and ground black pepper

COOK'S TIP
You can speed up this recipe by starting
the potatoes off in the microwave. Prick
the scrubbed potatoes well and place in
a covered microwave dish. Cook on high
until starting to soften – test after two
minutes, then every minute. Place in the
oven to crisp the skins and finish
cooking for about 45 minutes.

1 Preheat the oven to 200°C/400°F/
Gas 6. Scrub the potatoes and pat dry.
Prick each one with a fork and cook
directly on the middle shelf for 1 hour
20 minutes.

2 Remove the potatoes from the oven
and halve. Place the halves on a baking
sheet and make shallow dips in the
centre of each potato, raising the potato
up at the edges.

3 Mix the cheese and cream together
and divide between the potatoes.

4 Grill for 5 minutes until the cheese
has melted and started to bubble.
Serve hot, sprinkled with sea salt and
black pepper.

BOULANGÈRE POTATOES

*LAYERS OF POTATO AND ONIONS COOKED IN BUTTER AND STOCK. A DELICIOUS SAVOURY POTATO DISH
THAT MAKES A GREAT ACCOMPANIMENT TO BOTH MEAT AND FISH.*

SERVES SIX

INGREDIENTS
   butter for greasing
   450g/1lb maincrop potatoes, very
   finely sliced
   2 onions, finely sliced into rings
   2 garlic cloves, crushed
   50g/2oz/4 tbsp butter, diced
   300ml/½ pint/1¼ cups
   vegetable stock
   chopped parsley
   sea salt and ground black pepper

VARIATION
If you want to make this dish more
substantial, add some grated cheese,
sprinkled over the top just before you
bake it.

1 Preheat the oven to 180°C/350°F/
Gas 4. Grease the base and sides of a
1.5 litre/2½ pint/6¼ cup ovenproof dish.

2 Line the dish with some of the
sliced potatoes. Scatter some onions
and garlic on top. Layer up the
remaining potatoes and onions,
seasoning between each layer.

3 Push the vegetables down into the
dish and dot the top with the butter.
Pour the stock over and bake in the
oven for 1½ hours covering with foil
after 1 hour if the top starts to over
brown. Serve with parsley and plenty of
salt and pepper sprinkled over the top.

HERBY POTATO BAKE

WONDERFULLY CREAMY POTATOES WELL FLAVOURED WITH LOTS OF FRESH HERBS AND SPRINKLED WITH CHEESE TO MAKE A GOLDEN, CRUNCHY TOPPING.

SERVES FOUR

INGREDIENTS
   butter, for greasing
   675g/1½lb waxy potatoes
   25g/1oz/2 tbsp butter
   1 onion, finely chopped
   1 garlic clove, crushed
   2 eggs
   300ml/½ pint/1¼ cups crème fraîche
     or double cream
   115g/4oz/1 cup Gruyère, grated
   60ml/4 tbsp chopped mixed fresh
     herbs, such as chervil, thyme,
     chives and parsley
   freshly grated nutmeg
   salt and ground black pepper

1 Place a baking sheet in the oven and preheat to 190°C/375°F/Gas 5. Butter an ovenproof dish.

2 Peel the potatoes and cut them into matchsticks. Set aside while you make up the sauce mixture. Start by melting the butter in a pan and fry the onion and garlic until softened. Remove from the heat to cool slightly. In a large bowl, whisk together the eggs, crème fraîche or cream and about half of the grated Gruyère cheese.

3 Stir in the onion mixture, herbs, potatoes, salt, pepper and nutmeg. Spoon the mixture into the prepared dish and sprinkle over the remaining cheese. Bake on the hot baking sheet for 50 minutes to 1 hour until the top is golden brown. Serve immediately, straight from the dish, as this will ensure that the potatoes stay really hot.

OVEN CHIP ROASTIES

THIS EASY ALTERNATIVE TO FRIED CHIPS TASTES JUST AS GOOD AND IS MUCH EASIER TO COOK.

SERVES FOUR TO SIX

INGREDIENTS
   150ml/¼ pint/⅔ cup olive oil
   4 medium to large baking potatoes
   5ml/1 tsp mixed dried herbs
     (optional)
   sea salt flakes
   mayonnaise, to serve

VARIATION
Sweet potatoes also make fine oven chips. Prepare and roast in the same way as above, although you may find they do not take as long to cook.

COOK'S TIP
Oven chip roasties make great mid-week suppers served with fried eggs, mushrooms and tomatoes.

1 Preheat the oven to the highest temperature, generally 240°C/475°F/Gas 9. Lightly oil a large shallow roasting tin and place it in the oven to get really hot while you prepare the potatoes.

2 Cut the potatoes in half lengthwise, then into long thin wedges, or thicker ones if you prefer. Brush each side lightly with oil.

3 When the oven is really hot, remove the pan carefully and scatter the potato wedges over it, spreading them out in a single layer over the hot oil.

4 Sprinkle the potato wedges with the herbs and salt and roast for about 20 minutes, or longer if they are thicker, until they are golden brown, crisp and lightly puffy. Remove from the oven and serve with a dollop of mayonnaise.

GARLIC MASHED POTATOES

THESE CREAMY MASHED POTATOES ARE DELICIOUS WITH ALL KINDS OF ROAST OR SAUTÉED MEATS AS WELL AS VEGETARIAN MAIN DISHES AND ALTHOUGH IT SEEMS LIKE A LOT OF GARLIC, THE FLAVOUR TURNS SWEET AND SUBTLE WHEN COOKED IN THIS WAY.

SERVES SIX TO EIGHT

INGREDIENTS
  3 whole garlic bulbs, separated into
    cloves, unpeeled
  115g/4oz/8 tbsp unsalted butter
  1.5kg/3lb baking potatoes, quartered
  120–175ml/4–6fl oz/½–¾ cup milk
  salt and ground white pepper

COOK'S TIP
This recipe makes a very light, creamy
purée. Use less milk to achieve a firmer
purée, more for a softer purée. Be sure
the milk is almost boiling or it will cool
the potato mixture. Keep the purée warm
in a bowl over simmering water.

1 Bring a small saucepan of water to
the boil over a high heat. Add two thirds
of the garlic cloves and boil for
2 minutes. Drain the pan and then peel
the garlic cloves.

2 Place the remaining garlic cloves in
a roasting tin and bake in a preheated
oven at 200°C/400°F/Gas 6 for
30–40 minutes.

3 In a heavy-based frying pan, melt
50g/2oz/4 tbsp of the butter over a
low heat. Add the blanched garlic
cloves, then cover and cook gently for
20–25 minutes until very tender and
just golden, shaking the pan and
stirring occasionally. Do not allow the
garlic to scorch or brown.

4 Remove the pan from the heat and
cool. Spoon the garlic and melted butter
into a blender or a food processor fitted
with the metal blade and process until
smooth. Tip into a bowl, press clear film
on to the surface to prevent a skin
forming and set aside.

5 Cook the potatoes in boiling salted
water until tender, then drain and pass
through a food mill or press through a
sieve back into the saucepan. Return
the pan to a medium heat and, using
a wooden spoon, stir the potatoes for
1–2 minutes to dry out completely.
Remove the pan from the heat.

6 Warm the milk over a medium-high
heat until bubbles form around the
edge. Gradually beat the milk,
remaining butter and garlic purée into
the potatoes. Season with salt, if
needed, and white pepper, and serve
hot, with the roasted garlic cloves.

CHAMP

SIMPLE BUT UNBELIEVABLY TASTY, THIS TRADITIONAL IRISH WAY WITH MASHED POTATOES MAKES AN EXCELLENT COMPANION FOR A HEARTY STEW OF LAMB OR BEEF.

SERVES FOUR

INGREDIENTS

900g/2lb floury potatoes
1 small bunch spring onions,
    finely chopped
150ml/¼ pint/⅔ cup milk
50g/2oz/4 tbsp butter
salt and ground black pepper

COOK'S TIP
If you make too much mashed potato, don't worry. It keeps well in the fridge and simply needs re-heating.

1 Cut the potatoes up into large chunks. Place in a large pan and cook in boiling water for 20 minutes until tender.

2 Meanwhile put the spring onions into a saucepan with the milk. Bring to the boil then reduce the heat and simmer until the spring onions are just tender.

3 Drain the potatoes well and leave to cool. When they are cool enough to handle, peel and return to the saucepan. Put the pan on the heat and, using a wooden spoon, stir for 1 minute until the moisture has evaporated. Remove the pan from the heat.

4 Mash the potatoes with the milk and spring onions and season. Serve hot with a pool of melted butter in each portion.

PERFECT CREAMED POTATOES

REAL CREAMED POTATOES ARE A SIMPLE LUXURY YOU WILL FIND IN ANY FASHIONABLE RESTAURANT TODAY BUT ARE SO EASY TO MAKE AT HOME AS WELL.

SERVES FOUR

INGREDIENTS
 900g/2lb firm but not waxy
  potatoes, diced
 45ml/3 tbsp extra virgin olive oil
 about 150ml/¼ pint/⅔ cup hot milk
 freshly grated nutmeg
 a few fresh basil leaves or parsley
  sprigs, chopped
 salt and ground black pepper
 basil leaves, to garnish
 fried bacon, to serve

COOK'S TIP
Choosing the right variety of potato makes all the difference to this dish. A waxy potato won't be light and fluffy, and a potato which breaks down too quickly on boiling will become a slurry.

1 Cook the potatoes in boiling water until just tender but not too mushy. Drain very well. Press the potatoes through a special potato "ricer" (rather like a large garlic press) or mash them well with a potato masher. Do not use a food processor as it can give the potatoes a gluey consistency.

2 Beat in olive oil and enough hot milk to make a smooth, thick purée.

3 Flavour to taste with the nutmeg and seasoning, then stir in the chopped fresh herbs. Spoon into a warm serving dish and serve at once, garnished with basil leaves and fried bacon.

POTATOES WITH RED CHILLIES

IF YOU LIKE CHILLIES, YOU'LL LOVE THESE POTATOES! IF YOU'RE NOT A FAN OF FIERY FLAVOURS, THEN SIMPLY LEAVE OUT ALL THE CHILLI SEEDS AND USE THE FLESH BY ITSELF.

SERVES FOUR

INGREDIENTS
 12–14 small new or salad
  potatoes, halved
 30ml/2 tbsp vegetable oil
 2.5ml/½ tsp crushed dried
  red chillies
 2.5ml/½ tsp white cumin seeds
 2.5ml/½ tsp fennel seeds
 2.5ml/½ tsp crushed coriander seeds
 5ml/1 tsp salt
 1 onion, sliced
 1–4 fresh red chillies, chopped
 15ml/1 tbsp chopped fresh coriander
 chopped fresh coriander, to garnish

COOK'S TIP
To prepare fresh chillies, slit down one side and scrape out the seeds, unless you want a really hot dish. Finely slice or chop the flesh. Wear rubber gloves if you have very sensitive skin.

1 Cook the potatoes in boiling salted water until tender but still firm. Remove from the heat and drain off the water. Set aside until needed.

2 In a deep frying pan, heat the oil over a medium-high heat, then reduce the heat to medium. Add the crushed chillies, cumin, fennel and coriander seeds and salt and fry, stirring, for 30–40 seconds.

3 Add the sliced onion and fry until golden brown. Then add the potatoes, red chillies and coriander and stir well.

4 Reduce the heat to very low, then cover and cook for 5–7 minutes. Serve the potatoes hot, garnished with more fresh coriander.

HASH BROWNS

CRISPY GOLDEN WEDGES OF POTATOES, "HASHED" UP WITH A LITTLE ONION, ARE A FAVOURITE AMERICAN BREAKFAST DISH, BUT TASTE DELICIOUS ANYTIME.

SERVES 4

INGREDIENTS
   60ml/4 tbsp sunflower or olive oil
   450g/1lb cooked potatoes, diced
      or grated
   1 small onion, chopped
   salt and ground black pepper
   chives, to garnish
   tomato sauce, to serve

VARIATION

Turn this side dish into a main meal by adding other ingredients to the potatoes in the pan, such as cooked diced meat, sliced sausages or even corned beef for a northern English corned beef hash supper.

1 Heat the oil in a large heavy-based frying pan until very hot. Add the potatoes in a single layer. Scatter the onion on top and season well.

2 Cook on a medium heat, pressing down on the potatoes with a spoon or spatula to squash them together.

3 When the potatoes are nicely browned underneath, turn them over in sections with a spatula and fry until the other side is golden brown and lightly crispy, pressing them down again.

4 Serve hot with a garnish of chives and tomato sauce alongside.

SPANISH CHILLI POTATOES

THE NAME OF THIS SPANISH TAPAS DISH, "PATATAS BRAVAS", MEANS FIERCELY HOT POTATOES, BUT LUCKILY TAPAS ARE USUALLY ONLY EATEN IN SMALL QUANTITIES!

SERVES FOUR

INGREDIENTS
   900g/2lb small new or salad potatoes
   60ml/4 tbsp olive oil
   1 onion, finely chopped
   2 garlic cloves, crushed
   15ml/1 tbsp tomato paste
   200g/7oz can chopped tomatoes
   15ml/1 tbsp red wine vinegar
   2–3 small dried red chillies, seeded
      and finely chopped, or 5–10ml/
      1–2 tsp hot chilli powder
   5ml/1 tsp paprika
   salt and ground black pepper
   1 flat leaf parsley sprig, to garnish
   chopped fresh red chillies, to garnish

COOK'S TIP

If you don't like your potatoes to be too hot simply reduce the amount of chilli to taste.

1 Cook the potatoes in their skins in boiling water for 10–12 minutes until just tender. Drain well and leave to cool, then cut in half and reserve.

2 Heat the oil in a large pan and add the onion and garlic. Fry them gently for 5–6 minutes until just softened. Stir in the tomato paste, tomatoes, vinegar, chillies or chilli powder and paprika and simmer for about 5 minutes.

3 Stir the potatoes into the sauce mixture until well coated. Cover and simmer gently for 8–10 minutes until the potatoes are tender.

4 Season the potatoes well and transfer to a warmed serving dish. Serve at once, garnished with a sprig of flat leaf parsley. To make the dish even hotter, add a garnish of chopped fresh red chillies.

MASALA MASHED POTATOES

THESE WELL-SPICED POTATOES ARE DELICIOUS SERVED ALONGSIDE RICH MEATS SUCH AS DUCK,
LAMB OR PORK THAT HAS BEEN SIMPLY GRILLED OR ROASTED.

SERVES FOUR

INGREDIENTS
    3 medium floury potatoes
    15ml/1 tbsp mixed chopped fresh
        mint and coriander
    5ml/1 tsp mango powder or chutney
    5ml/1 tsp salt
    5ml/1 tsp crushed black peppercorns
    1 fresh red chilli, finely chopped
    1 fresh green chilli, finely chopped
    50g/2oz/4 tbsp butter or
        margarine, softened

1 Cook the potatoes in a large pan of lightly salted boiling water until tender. Drain very well. Mash them well with a potato masher.

2 Blend together the remaining ingredients in a small bowl.

3 Stir the mixture into the mashed potatoes reserving a little for a garnish and mix together with a fork.

4 Serve hot in a pile, with the remaining mixture on the top.

BOMBAY POTATOES

A CLASSIC GUJERATI (INDIAN VEGETARIAN) DISH OF POTATOES SLOWLY COOKED IN A RICHLY
FLAVOURED CURRY SAUCE WITH FRESH CHILLIES FOR AN ADDED KICK.

SERVES FOUR TO SIX

INGREDIENTS
    450g/1lb new or small salad potatoes
    5ml/1 tsp turmeric
    60ml/4 tbsp vegetable oil
    2 dried red chillies
    6–8 curry leaves
    2 onions, finely chopped
    2 fresh green chillies, finely chopped
    50g/2oz coriander leaves,
        coarsely chopped
    1.5ml/¼ tsp asafoetida
    2.5ml/½ tsp each cumin, mustard,
        onion, fennel and nigella seeds
    lemon juice
    salt
    fresh fried curry leaves, to garnish

1 Chop the potatoes into small chunks and cook in boiling lightly salted water with ½ tsp of the turmeric until tender. Drain, then coarsely mash. Set aside.

2 Heat the oil in a large heavy-based pan and fry the red chillies and curry leaves until the chillies are nearly burnt. Add the onions, green chillies, coriander, remaining turmeric, asafoetida and spice seeds and cook until the onions are tender.

3 Fold in the potatoes and add a few drops of water. Cook on a low heat for about 10 minutes, mixing well to ensure the even distribution of the spices. Remove the dried chillies and curry leaves.

4 Serve the potatoes hot, with lemon juice squeezed or poured over, and garnish with the fresh fried curry leaves, if you wish.

Meat and Poultry Dishes

These meat and poultry dishes make the most of the potatoes in season throughout the year. Lamb shanks slowly cooked in spices are finished with halved new potatoes. Chicken in a light sauce is topped with herby dumplings made with mashed potatoes, and a rich beef dish is finished with a crispy grated potato crust.

TEX-MEX BAKED POTATOES WITH CHILLI

CLASSIC CHILLI MINCE TOPS CRISP, FLOURY-CENTRED BAKED POTATOES. EASY TO PREPARE AND GREAT FOR A SIMPLE, YET SUBSTANTIAL FAMILY SUPPER.

SERVES FOUR

INGREDIENTS
  2 large baking potatoes
  15ml/1 tbsp vegetable oil, plus more
    for brushing
  1 garlic clove, crushed
  1 small onion, chopped
  ½ red pepper, seeded and chopped
  225g/8oz lean beef mince
  ½ small fresh red chilli, seeded
    and chopped
  5ml/1 tsp ground cumin
  pinch of cayenne pepper
  200g/7oz can chopped tomatoes
  30ml/2 tbsp tomato paste
  2.5ml/½ tsp fresh oregano
  2.5ml/½ tsp fresh marjoram
  200g/7oz can red kidney beans,
    drained
  15ml/1 tbsp chopped fresh coriander
  salt and ground black pepper
  chopped fresh marjoram, to garnish
  lettuce leaves, to serve
  60ml/4 tbsp soured cream, to serve

1 Preheat the oven to 220°C/425°F/
Gas 7. Brush or rub the potatoes with a
little of the oil and then pierce them
with skewers.

2 Place the potatoes on the top shelf
of the oven and bake them for
30 minutes before beginning to
cook the chilli.

3 Heat the oil in a large heavy pan and
add the garlic, onion and pepper. Fry
gently for 4–5 minutes until softened.

4 Add the beef and fry until browned,
then stir in the chilli, cumin, cayenne
pepper, tomatoes, tomato paste,
60ml/4 tbsp water and the herbs. Bring
to a boil then reduce the heat, cover
and simmer for about 25 minutes,
stirring occasionally.

5 Stir in the kidney beans and cook,
uncovered, for 5 minutes. Remove from
the heat and stir in the chopped
coriander. Season well and set aside.

6 Cut the baked potatoes in half and
place them in serving bowls. Top with
the chilli mixture and a dollop of soured
cream. Garnish with chopped fresh
marjoram and serve hot accompanied
by a few lettuce leaves.

CORNED BEEF AND EGG HASH

THIS IS REAL NURSERY, OR COMFORT, FOOD AT ITS BEST! WHETHER YOU REMEMBER GRAN'S VERSION, OR PREFER THIS AMERICAN-STYLE HASH, IT TURNS CORNED BEEF INTO A SUPPER FIT FOR ANY GUEST.

SERVES FOUR

INGREDIENTS
    30ml/2 tbsp vegetable oil
    25g/1oz/2 tbsp butter
    1 onion, finely chopped
    1 green pepper, seeded and diced
    2 large firm boiled potatoes, diced
    350g/12oz can corned beef, cubed
    1.5ml/¼ tsp grated nutmeg
    1.5ml/¼ tsp paprika
    4 eggs
    salt and ground black pepper
    deep fried parsley, to garnish
    sweet chilli sauce or tomato sauce,
        to serve

COOK'S TIP
Put the can of corned beef into the fridge to chill for about half an hour before using – it will firm up and cut into cubes more easily.

1 Heat the oil and butter together in a large frying pan. Add the onion and fry for 5–6 minutes until softened.

2 In a bowl, mix together the green pepper, potatoes, corned beef, nutmeg and paprika and season well. Add to the pan and toss gently to distribute the cooked onion. Press down lightly and fry without stirring on a medium heat for about 3–4 minutes until a golden brown crust has formed on the underside.

3 Stir the mixture through to distribute the crust, then repeat the frying twice, until the mixture is well browned.

4 Make four wells in the hash and carefully crack an egg into each. Cover and cook gently for about 4–5 minutes until the egg whites are set.

5 Sprinkle with deep fried parsley and cut into quarters. Serve hot with sweet chilli sauce or tomato sauce.

SLOW BAKED BEEF WITH A POTATO CRUST

THIS RECIPE MAKES THE BEST OF BRAISING BEEF BY MARINATING IT IN RED WINE AND TOPPING IT WITH A CHEESY GRATED POTATO CRUST THAT BAKES TO A GOLDEN, CRUNCHY CONSISTENCY. FOR A CHANGE, INSTEAD OF GRATING THE POTATOES, SLICE THEM THINLY AND LAYER OVER THE TOP OF THE BEEF WITH ONION RINGS AND CRUSHED GARLIC.

SERVES FOUR

INGREDIENTS
  675g/1½lb stewing beef, diced
  300ml/½ pint/1¼ cups red wine
  3 juniper berries, crushed
  slice of orange peel
  30ml/2 tbsp olive oil
  2 onions, cut into chunks
  2 carrots, cut into chunks
  1 garlic clove, crushed
  225g/8oz/3 cups button
    mushrooms
  150ml/¼ pint/⅔ cup beef stock
  30ml/2 tbsp cornflour
  salt and ground black pepper
For the crust
  450g/1lb potatoes, grated
  15ml/1 tbsp olive oil
  30ml/2 tbsp creamed horseradish
  50g/2oz/½ cup mature Cheddar
    cheese, grated
  salt and ground black pepper

VARIATION
Any hard mature cheese is suitable for cooking on the crust. Try Red Leicester to add some colour, or Munster, for a more pungent flavour.

1 Place the diced beef in a non-metallic bowl. Add the wine, berries, and orange peel and season with black pepper. Mix the ingredients together and then cover and leave to marinate for at least 4 hours or overnight if possible.

2 Preheat the oven to 160°C/325°F/Gas 3. Drain the beef, reserving the marinade.

3 Heat the oil in a large flameproof casserole and fry the meat in batches for 5 minutes to seal. Add the onions, carrots and garlic and cook for 5 minutes. Stir in the mushrooms, red wine marinade and beef stock. Simmer.

4 Mix the cornflour with water to make a smooth paste. Stir into the pan. Season, cover and cook for 1½ hours.

5 Make the crust 30 minutes before the end of the cooking time for the beef. Start by blanching the grated potatoes in boiling water for 5 minutes. Drain well and then squeeze out all the extra liquid.

6 Stir in the remaining ingredients and then scatter evenly over the surface of the beef. Increase the oven temperature to 200°C/400°F/Gas 6 and cook the dish for a further 30 minutes so that the top is crispy and slightly browned.

COOK'S TIP
Use a large grater on the food processor for the potatoes. They will hold their shape better whilst being blanched than if you use a finer blade.

MOUSSAKA

THIS CLASSIC GREEK DISH WITH LAMB, POTATOES AND AUBERGINES IS LAYERED THROUGH WITH A RICH CHEESY TOPPING TO MAKE A SUBSTANTIAL MEAL.

SERVES SIX

INGREDIENTS
  30ml/2 tbsp olive oil
  30ml/2 tbsp chopped
    fresh oregano
  1 large onion, finely chopped
  675g/1½lb lean lamb, minced
  1 large aubergine, sliced
  2 x 400g/14oz cans
    chopped tomatoes
  45ml/3 tbsp tomato purée
  1 lamb stock cube, crumbled
  2 floury main crop
    potatoes, halved
  115g/4oz/1 cup Cheddar
    cheese, grated
  150ml/¼ pint/⅔ cup
    single cream
  salt and ground black pepper
  fresh bread, to serve

1 Preheat the oven to 180°C/350°F/ Gas 4. Heat the olive oil in a large deep-sided frying pan. Fry the oregano and onions over a low heat, stirring frequently, for about 5 minutes or until the onions have softened.

VARIATION
If you want to add more vegetables to the dish, use slices of courgette, grilled in the same way as the aubergines, instead of the sliced potato in the layers, then top the dish with a layer of well-seasoned mashed potatoes before pouring over the sauce. To make the dish even richer, add a sprinkling of freshly grated Parmesan cheese with each layer of aubergine.

2 Stir in the lamb and cook for 10 minutes until browned. Meanwhile, grill the aubergine slices for 5 minutes until browned, turning once.

3 Stir the tomatoes and purée into the mince mixture, and crumble the stock cube over it, stir well, season with salt and pepper and simmer uncovered for a further 15 minutes.

4 Meanwhile, cook the potatoes in lightly salted boiling water for 5–10 minutes until just tender. Drain, and when cool enough to handle, cut into thin slices.

5 Layer the aubergines, mince and potatoes in a 1.75 litre/3 pint/7½ cup oval ovenproof dish, finishing with a layer of potatoes.

6 Mix the cheese and cream together in a bowl and pour over the top of the other ingredients in the dish. Cook for 45–50 minutes until bubbling and golden on the top. Serve straight from the dish, while hot, with plenty of fresh, crusty bread.

COOK'S TIP
The larger the surface area of the dish, the quicker the Moussaka will cook in the oven.

IRISH STEW

SIMPLE AND DELICIOUS, THIS IS THE QUINTESSENTIAL IRISH MAIN COURSE. TRADITIONALLY MUTTON CHOPS ARE USED, BUT AS THEY ARE HARDER TO FIND THESE DAYS YOU CAN USE LAMB INSTEAD.

SERVES FOUR

INGREDIENTS
1.5kg/2½lb boneless lamb chops
15ml/1 tbsp vegetable oil
3 large onions, quartered
4 large carrots, thickly sliced
900ml/1½ pints/3¾ cups water
4 large firm potatoes, cut into chunks
1 large thyme sprig
15g/½oz/1 tbsp butter
15ml/1 tbsp chopped fresh parsley
salt and ground black pepper
Savoy cabbage, to serve (optional)

COOK'S TIP
If you can't find boneless chops, use the same weight of middle neck of lamb. Ask the butcher to chop the meat into cutlets, which should then be trimmed of excess fat.

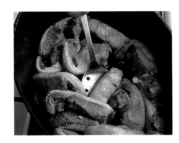

1 Trim any excess fat from the lamb. Heat the oil in a flameproof casserole, add the lamb and brown on both sides. Remove from the pan.

2 Add the onions and carrots to the casserole and cook for 5 minutes until the onions are browned. Return the lamb to the pan with the water. Season with salt and pepper. Bring to a boil then reduce the heat, cover and simmer for 1 hour.

3 Add the potatoes to the pan with the thyme, cover again, and simmer for a further hour.

4 Leave the stew to settle for a few minutes. Remove the fat from the liquid with a ladle, then pour off the liquid into a clean saucepan. Bring to a simmer and stir in the butter, then the parsley. Season well and pour back into the casserole. Serve with Savoy cabbage, boiled or steamed, if liked.

MIDDLE EASTERN ROAST LAMB AND POTATOES

WHEN THE EASTERN AROMA OF THE GARLIC AND SAFFRON COME WAFTING OUT OF THE OVEN, THIS DELICIOUSLY GARLICKY LAMB WON'T LAST VERY LONG!

SERVES SIX TO EIGHT

INGREDIENTS
2.75kg/6lb leg of lamb
4 garlic cloves, halved
60ml/4 tbsp olive oil
juice of 1 lemon
2–3 saffron strands, soaked in
    15ml/1 tbsp boiling water
5ml/1 tsp mixed dried herbs
450g/1lb baking potatoes,
    thickly sliced
2 large onions, thickly sliced
salt and ground black pepper
fresh thyme, to garnish

1 Make eight incisions in the lamb, press the garlic into the slits and place the lamb in a non-metallic dish.

2 Mix together the oil, lemon juice, saffron mixture and herbs. Rub over the lamb and marinate for 2 hours.

3 Preheat the oven to 180°C/350°F/ Gas 4. Layer the potatoes and onions in a large roasting tin. Lift the lamb out of the marinade and place the lamb on top of the potatoes and onions, fat side up and season.

4 Pour any remaining marinade over the lamb and roast for 2 hours, basting occasionally. Remove from the oven, cover with foil and rest for 10–15 minutes before carving. Garnish with thyme.

LAMB AND NEW POTATO CURRY

THIS DISH MAKES THE MOST OF AN ECONOMICAL CUT OF MEAT BY COOKING IT SLOWLY UNTIL THE MEAT IS FALLING FROM THE BONE. CHILLIES AND COCONUT CREAM GIVE IT LOTS OF FLAVOUR.

SERVES FOUR

INGREDIENTS
  25g/1oz/2 tbsp butter
  4 garlic cloves, crushed
  2 onions, sliced into rings
  2.5ml/½ tsp each ground cumin,
    ground coriander, turmeric and
    cayenne pepper
  2–3 red chillies, seeded and
    finely chopped
  300ml/½ pint/1¼ cups hot
    chicken stock
  200ml/7fl oz/scant 1 cup
    coconut cream
  4 lamb shanks, all excess
    fat removed
  450g/1lb new potatoes, halved
  6 ripe tomatoes, quartered
  salt and ground black pepper
  coriander leaves, to garnish
  spicy rice, to serve

2 Stir in the hot stock and coconut cream. Place the lamb shanks in the liquid and cover the casserole with foil. Cook in the oven for 2 hours, turning the shanks twice, first after about an hour or so and again about half an hour later.

3 Par-boil the potatoes for 10 minutes, drain and add to the casserole with the tomatoes, then cook uncovered in the oven for a further 35 minutes. Season to taste and garnish with coriander leaves and serve with the spicy rice.

1 Preheat the oven to 160°C/325°F/Gas 3. Melt the butter in a large flameproof casserole, add the garlic and onions and cook over a low heat for 15 minutes, until golden. Stir in the spices and chillies, then cook for a further 2 minutes.

COOK'S TIP
Make this dish a day in advance if possible. Cool and chill overnight, then skim off the excess fat that has risen to the surface. Reheat thoroughly before you serve it.

POTATO AND SAUSAGE CASSEROLE

YOU WILL FIND NUMEROUS VARIATIONS OF THIS TRADITIONAL SUPPER DISH THROUGHOUT IRELAND,
BUT THE BASIC INGREDIENTS ARE THE SAME WHEREVER YOU GO — POTATOES, SAUSAGES AND BACON.

SERVES FOUR

INGREDIENTS
    15ml/1 tbsp vegetable oil
    4 bacon rashers, cut into
    2.5cm/1in pieces
    2 large onions, chopped
    2 garlic cloves, crushed
    8 large pork sausages
    4 large baking potatoes, thinly sliced
    1.5ml/¼ tsp fresh sage
    300ml/½ pint/1¼ cups
    vegetable stock
    salt and ground black pepper
    soda bread, to serve

1 Preheat the oven to 180°C/350°F/
Gas 4. Grease a large ovenproof dish
and set aside.

2 Heat the oil in a frying pan. Add the
bacon and fry for 2 minutes. Add the
onions and fry for 5–6 minutes until
golden. Add the garlic and fry for
1 minute, then remove the mixture
from the pan and set aside.

3 Then fry the sausages in the pan for
5–6 minutes until golden brown.

4 Arrange the potatoes in the base of
the prepared dish. Spoon the bacon
and onion mixture on top. Season with
the salt and pepper and sprinkle with
the fresh sage.

5 Pour on the stock and top with the
sausages. Cover and bake for 1 hour.
Serve hot with fresh soda bread.

WILD MUSHROOM AND BACON RÖSTI

*DRIED CEPS OR PORCINI MUSHROOMS HAVE A WONDERFUL WOODY, EARTHY AROMA AND TASTE.
WITH THE SALTY BACON LARDONS, THEY TURN POTATO RÖSTI INTO A MEMORABLE SUPPER.*

SERVES FOUR

INGREDIENTS
675g/1½ lb floury potatoes
10g/¼ oz dried ceps or porcini
  mushrooms
225g/8oz very thick smoked bacon,
  cut into lardons or strips
2 thyme sprigs, chopped
30ml/2 tbsp chopped fresh parsley
30ml/2 tbsp vegetable oil
4 eggs, to serve
1 bunch watercress, to garnish
crushed peppercorns, to garnish

1 Cook the potatoes in a saucepan of boiling salted water for 5 minutes and not longer, as they need to remain firm enough to grate at the next stage.

2 Meanwhile cover the mushrooms with boiling water and leave to soften for 5–10 minutes. Drain and chop.

3 Fry the bacon gently in a non-stick pan until all the fat runs out. Remove the bacon using a slotted spoon and reserve the fat.

4 Drain the potatoes and leave to cool. When they are cool enough to handle, grate them coarsely, then thoroughly pat dry on kitchen paper to remove all moisture. Place them in a large bowl and add the mushrooms, thyme, parsley and bacon. Mix together well.

5 Heat the bacon fat with a little of the oil in the frying pan until really hot. Spoon in the rösti mixture in heaps and flatten. Fry in batches for about 6 minutes until crisp and golden on both sides, turning once. Drain on kitchen paper and keep warm in a low oven.

6 Heat the remaining oil in the hot pan and fry the eggs as you like them. Serve the rösti at once with the eggs, watercress and crushed peppercorns.

POTATO CHORIZO AND CHEESE TORTILLA

SLICED POTATOES AND CHILLI-HOT SAUSAGES MAKE A POTATO CAKE WITH A REAL KICK TO IT.

SERVES FOUR

INGREDIENTS
15ml/1 tbsp vegetable oil
½ onion, sliced
1 small green pepper, seeded and cut
  into rings
1 garlic clove, finely chopped
1 tomato, chopped
6 pitted black olives, chopped
275g/10oz cooked firm, waxy
  potatoes, sliced
225g/8oz sliced chorizo, in strips
1 fresh green chilli, seeded
  and chopped
50g/2oz/½ cup Cheddar
  cheese, grated
6 large eggs
45ml/3 tbsp milk
1.5ml/¼ tsp ground cumin
1.5ml/¼ tsp dried oregano
1.5ml/¼ tsp paprika
salt and ground black pepper
rocket leaves, to garnish

1 Preheat the oven to 190°C/375°F/ Gas 5. Line a 23cm/9in round cake tin with grease-proof paper.

2 Heat the oil in a large non-stick frying pan. Add the onion, green pepper and garlic and cook over a medium heat for 5–8 minutes until softened.

3 Spoon into the tin with the tomato, olives, potatoes, chorizo and chilli. Mix and sprinkle with cheese.

4 In a small bowl, whisk together the eggs and milk until frothy. Add the cumin, oregano, paprika and salt and pepper to taste. Whisk to blend.

5 Pour the egg mixture on to the vegetables, tilting the tin so that the egg mixture spreads evenly.

6 Bake for 30 minutes until set and lightly golden. Serve in wedges, hot or cold, with rocket leaves.

PORK ESCALOPES BAKED WITH APPLE AND POTATO RÖSTI

THE JUICES FROM THE PORK COOK INTO THE APPLES AND POTATOES GIVING THEM A WONDERFUL FLAVOUR AS WELL AS MAKING A DELICIOUS SAUCE.

SERVES FOUR

INGREDIENTS

  2 large potatoes, finely grated
  1 medium Bramley apple, grated
  2 garlic cloves, crushed
  1 egg, beaten
  butter, for greasing
  15ml/1 tbsp olive oil
  4 large slices Parma ham
  4 pork escalopes, about
    175g/6oz each
  4 sage leaves
  1 medium Bramley apple,
    cut into thin wedges
  25g/1oz/2 tbsp butter, diced
  salt and ground black pepper
  caramelized apple wedges, to serve

COOK'S TIP
Do not be tempted to overcook the pork as it will start to dry out.

1 Preheat the oven to 200°C/400°F/ Gas 6. Squeeze out all the excess liquid from the grated potatoes and apple. Mix the grated ingredients together with the garlic, egg and seasoning.

2 Divide the potatoes into 4 portions and spoon each quarter on to a baking sheet that has been lined with foil and greased. Form a circle with the potatoes and flatten out slightly with the back of a spoon. Drizzle with a little olive oil. Cook for 10 minutes.

3 Meanwhile, lay the Parma ham on a clean surface and place a pork escalope on top. Lay a sage leaf and apple wedges over each escalope and top each piece with the butter. Wrap the Parma ham around each piece of meat, making sure it is covered completely.

4 Remove the potatoes from the oven, place each pork parcel on top and return to the oven for 20 minutes. Carefully lift the pork and potatoes off the foil and serve with caramelized wedges of apple and any cooking juices on the side.

TURKEY CROQUETTES

A CRISP PATTY OF SMOKED TURKEY MIXED WITH MASHED POTATO AND SPRING ONIONS AND ROLLED IN BREADCRUMBS, SERVED WITH A TANGY TOMATO SAUCE.

3 Meanwhile, to make the sauce heat the oil in a frying pan and fry the onion for 5 minutes until softened. Add the tomatoes and purée, stir and simmer for 10 minutes. Stir in the parsley, season with salt and pepper and keep the sauce warm until needed.

SERVES FOUR

INGREDIENTS
    450g/1lb main crop potatoes,diced
    3 eggs
    30ml/2 tbsp milk
    175g/6oz smoked turkey rashers,
      finely chopped
    2 spring onions, finely sliced
    115g/4oz/2 cups fresh white
      breadcrumbs
    vegetable oil, for deep fat frying
For the sauce
    15ml/1 tbsp olive oil
    1 onion, finely chopped
    400g/14oz can tomatoes, drained
    30ml/2 tbsp tomato purée
    15ml/1 tbsp chopped fresh parsley
    salt and ground black pepper

1 Boil the potatoes for 20 minutes or until tender. Drain and return the pan to a low heat to make sure all the excess water evaporates.

2 Mash the potatoes with 2 eggs and the milk. Season well with salt and pepper. Stir in the turkey and spring onions. Chill for 1 hour.

4 Remove the potato mixture from the fridge and divide into 8 pieces. Shape each piece into a sausage shape and dip in the remaining beaten egg and then the breadcrumbs.

5 Heat the vegetable oil in a saucepan or deep-fat fryer to 175°C/330°F and deep fry the croquettes for 5 minutes, or until golden and crisp. Serve with the sauce.

COOK'S TIP
Test the oil is at the correct temperature by dropping a cube of bread on to the surface. If it sinks, rises and sizzles in 10 seconds the oil is ready to use.

CHICKEN WITH POTATO DUMPLINGS

POACHED CHICKEN BREAST IN A CREAMY SAUCE TOPPED WITH LIGHT HERB AND POTATO DUMPLINGS
MAKES A DELICATE YET HEARTY AND WARMING MEAL.

SERVES SIX

INGREDIENTS
   1 onion, chopped
   300ml/½ pint/1¼ cups
     vegetable stock
   120ml/4fl oz/½ cup white wine
   4 large chicken breasts
   300ml/½ pint/1¼ cups single cream
   15ml/1 tbsp chopped fresh tarragon
   salt and ground black pepper
For the dumplings
   225g/8oz main crop potatoes, boiled
     and mashed
   175g/6oz/1¼ cups suet
   115g/4oz/1 cup self-raising flour
   50ml/2fl oz/¼ cup water
   30ml/2 tbsp chopped mixed
     fresh herbs
   salt and ground black pepper

1 Place the onion, stock and wine in a deep-sided frying pan. Add the chicken and simmer for 20 minutes, covered.

2 Remove the chicken from the stock, cut into chunks and reserve. Strain the stock and discard the onion. Reduce the stock by one-third over a high heat. Stir in the cream and tarragon and simmer until just thickened. Stir in the chicken and season with salt and ground black pepper.

3 Spoon the mixture into a 900ml/ 1½ pint/3¾ cup ovenproof dish.

4 Preheat the oven to 190°C/375°F/ Gas 5. Mix together the dumpling ingredients and stir in the water to make a soft dough. Divide into six and shape into balls with floured hands. Place on top of the chicken mixture and bake uncovered for 30 minutes.

COOK'S TIP
Make sure that you do not reduce the sauce too much before it is cooked in the oven as the dumplings absorb quite a lot of the liquid.

SPINACH AND POTATO STUFFED CHICKEN BREASTS

THIS DISH CONSISTS OF LARGE CHICKEN BREASTS, FILLED WITH A HERBY SPINACH MIXTURE, THEN TOPPED WITH BUTTER AND BAKED UNTIL MOUTH-WATERINGLY TENDER.

2 Stir the spinach into the potato with the egg and coriander. Season with salt and pepper to taste.

3 Cut almost all the way through the chicken breasts and open out to form a pocket in each. Spoon the filling into the centre and fold the chicken back over again. Secure with cocktail sticks and place in a roasting tin.

4 Dot with butter and cover with foil. Bake for 25 minutes. Remove the foil and cook for a further 10 minutes until the chicken is golden.

5 Meanwhile, to make the sauce heat the tomatoes, garlic and stock in a saucepan. Boil rapidly for 10 minutes. Season and stir in the coriander. Remove the chicken from the oven and serve with the sauce and fried mushrooms.

COOK'S TIP
Young spinach leaves have a sweeter flavour and are ideal for this dish.

SERVES SIX

INGREDIENTS
115g/4oz floury main crop
  potatoes, diced
115g/4oz spinach leaves,
  finely chopped
1 egg, beaten
30ml/2 tbsp chopped fresh coriander
4 large chicken breasts
50g/2oz/4 tbsp butter
For the sauce
400g/14oz can chopped tomatoes
1 garlic clove, crushed
150ml/¼ pint/⅔ cup hot chicken stock
30ml/2 tbsp chopped fresh coriander
salt and ground black pepper
fried mushrooms, to serve

1 Preheat the oven to 180°C/350°F/ Gas 4. Boil the potatoes in a large saucepan of boiling water for 15 minutes or until tender. Drain the potatoes, place them in a large bowl and roughly mash with a fork.

LAYERED CHICKEN AND MUSHROOM POTATO BAKE

A DELICIOUS AND MOIST COMBINATION OF CHICKEN, VEGETABLES AND GRAVY IN A SIMPLE, ONE-DISH MEAL TOPPED WITH CRUNCHY SLICES OF POTATO.

SERVES FOUR TO SIX

INGREDIENTS
15ml/1 tbsp olive oil
4 large chicken breasts, cut
  into chunks
1 leek, finely sliced into rings
50g/2oz/4 tbsp butter
25g/1oz/¼ cup plain flour
475ml/16fl oz/2 cups milk
5ml/1 tsp wholegrain mustard
1 carrot, very finely diced
225g/8oz/3 cups button mushrooms,
  finely sliced
900g/2lb main crop potatoes,
  finely sliced
salt and ground black pepper

1 Preheat the oven to 180°C/350°F/
Gas 4. Heat the oil in a large saucepan.
Fry the chicken for 5 minutes until
browned. Add the leek and fry for a
further 5 minutes.

2 Add half the butter to the pan and
allow it to melt. Then sprinkle the flour
over and stir in the milk. Cook over a
low heat until thickened, then stir in
the mustard.

3 Add the carrots with the mushrooms.
Season with salt and black pepper.

4 Lay enough potato slices to line the
base of a 1.75 litre/3 pint/7½ cup
ovenproof dish. Spoon one-third of the
chicken mixture over. Cover with
another layer of potatoes. Repeat
layering, finishing with a layer of
potatoes. Top with the remaining butter
in knobs.

5 Bake for 1½ hours in the oven,
covering with foil after 30 minutes'
cooking time. Serve hot.

COOK'S TIP
The liquid from the mushrooms keeps
the chicken moist and the potatoes help
to mop up any excess juices.

ROASTED DUCKLING ON A BED OF HONEYED POTATOES

THE RICH FLAVOUR OF DUCK COMBINED WITH THESE SWEETENED POTATOES GLAZED WITH HONEY MAKES AN EXCELLENT TREAT FOR A DINNER PARTY OR SPECIAL OCCASION.

SERVES FOUR

INGREDIENTS

   1 duckling, giblets removed
   60ml/4 tbsp light soy sauce
   150ml/¼ pint/⅔ cup fresh
     orange juice
   3 large floury potatoes, cut
     into chunks
   30ml/2 tbsp clear honey
   15ml/1 tbsp sesame seeds
   salt and ground black pepper

1 Preheat the oven to 200°C/400°F/ Gas 6. Place the duckling in a roasting tin. Prick the skin well.

2 Mix the soy sauce and orange juice together and pour over the duck. Cook for 20 minutes.

3 Place the potato chunks in a bowl and stir in the honey, toss to mix well. Remove the duckling from the oven and spoon the potatoes all around and under the duckling.

4 Roast for 35 minutes and remove from the oven. Toss the potatoes in the juices so the underside will be cooked and turn the duck over. Put back in the oven and cook for a further 30 minutes.

5 Remove the duckling from the oven and carefully scoop off the excess fat, leaving the juices behind.

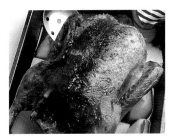

6 Sprinkle the sesame seeds over the potatoes, season and turn the duckling back over, breast side up, and cook for a further 10 minutes. Remove the duckling and potatoes from the oven and keep warm, allowing the duck to stand for a few minutes.

7 Pour off the excess fat and simmer the juices on the hob for a few minutes. Serve the juices with the carved duckling and potatoes.

Fish Dishes

FISH TAKES ONLY A SHORT TIME TO COOK, SO
MANY OF THE RECIPES IN THIS CHAPTER USE
POTATOES READY-COOKED OR VERY FINELY
SLICED. TRY JANSSON'S TEMPTATION, A
CLASSIC SWEDISH DISH MADE WITH
MATCHSTICK POTATOES AND LAYERED WITH
ANCHOVIES AND ONIONS. SINCE FISH LENDS
ITSELF WELL TO BEING FLAKED
IT IS IDEAL FOR MIXING
WITH MASHED POTATO
TO MAKE THE
TASTIEST OF
FISH CAKES.

SMOKED SALMON QUICHE WITH POTATO PASTRY

THE INGREDIENTS IN THIS LIGHT BUT RICHLY-FLAVOURED QUICHE PERFECTLY COMPLEMENT THE MELT-IN-THE-MOUTH PASTRY MADE WITH POTATOES.

SERVES SIX

INGREDIENTS
For the pastry
   115g/4oz floury maincrop
    potatoes, diced
   225g/8oz/2 cups plain flour, sifted
   115g/4oz/8 tbsp butter, diced
   ½ egg, beaten
   10ml/2 tsp chilled water
For the filling
   275g/10oz smoked salmon
   6 eggs, beaten
   150ml/¼ pint/⅔ cup full cream milk
   300ml/½ pint/1¼ cups double cream
   30–45ml/2–3 tbsp chopped fresh dill
   30ml/2 tbsp capers, chopped
   salt and ground black pepper
   salad leaves and chopped fresh dill,
    to serve

1 Boil the potatoes in a large saucepan of lightly salted water for 15 minutes or until tender. Drain well through a colander and return to the pan. Mash the potatoes until smooth and set aside to cool completely.

VARIATIONS
These quantities can also be used to make six individual quiches, which are an ideal size to serve as a starter or a light lunch. Prepare them as above, but reduce the cooking time by about 15 minutes. For extra piquancy, sprinkle some finely grated fresh Parmesan cheese over the top of each quiche before baking in the oven.

2 Place the flour in a bowl and rub in the butter to form fine crumbs. Beat in the potatoes and egg. Bring the mixture together, adding chilled water if needed.

3 Roll the pastry out on a floured surface and use to line a deep 23cm/9in round, loose-based, fluted flan tin. Chill for 1 hour.

4 Preheat the oven to 200°C/400°F/ Gas 6. Place a baking sheet in the oven to preheat it. Chop the salmon into bite-size pieces and set aside.

5 For the filling, beat the eggs, milk and cream together. Then stir in the dill and capers and season with pepper. Add in the salmon and stir to combine.

6 Remove the pastry case from the fridge, prick the base well and pour the mixture into it. Bake on a baking sheet for 35–45 minutes. Serve warm with mixed salad leaves and some more dill.

COOK'S TIPS
To ensure the base cooks through it is vital to preheat a baking sheet in the oven first. Make the most of smoked salmon offcuts for this quiche, as they are much cheaper.

TUNA AND MASCARPONE BAKE

A ONE-DISH MEAL IDEAL FOR INFORMAL ENTERTAINING THAT MARRIES THE SMOKY FLAVOUR OF SEARED TUNA WITH A SWEET AND HERBY ITALIAN SAUCE.

SERVES FOUR

INGREDIENTS
    4 x 175g/6oz tuna steaks
    400g/14oz can chopped
       tomatoes, drained
    2 garlic cloves, crushed
    30ml/2 tbsp chopped fresh basil
    250g/9oz/generous 1 cup
       mascarpone cheese
    3 large potatoes
    25g/1oz/2 tbsp butter, diced
    salt and ground black pepper

VARIATION
This dish can easily be made into a side dish, simply leave out the tuna and prepare the other ingredients as before.

1 Preheat the oven to 200°C/400°F/ Gas 6. Heat a griddle pan on the hob and sear the fish steaks for 2 minutes on each side, seasoning with a little black pepper. Set aside while you prepare the sauce.

2 Mix the tomatoes, garlic, basil and cheese together in a bowl and season to taste.

3 Grate half the potatoes and dice the other half. Blanch in separate pans of lightly salted water for 3 minutes. Drain.

4 Grease a 1.75 litre/3 pint/7½ cup ovenproof dish. Spoon a little sauce and some grated potato into it. Lay the tuna over with more sauce and the remaining grated potato. Scatter the diced butter and potatoes. Bake for 30 minutes.

POTATO AND SMOKED MUSSEL BAKE

THIS RECIPE USES SMOKED MUSSELS, WHICH HAVE A CREAMY TEXTURE AND RICH FLAVOUR, DELICIOUS WITH SOURED CREAM AND CHIVES. YOU CAN EASILY SUBSTITUTE SMOKED OYSTERS FOR THE MUSSELS.

SERVES FOUR

INGREDIENTS
    2 large maincrop potatoes,
       cut in half
    butter, for greasing
    2 shallots, finely diced
    2 x 85g/3¼oz tins smoked mussels
    1 bunch chives, snipped
    300ml/½ pint/1¼ cups soured cream
    175g/6oz/1½ cups mature Cheddar
       cheese, grated
    salt and ground black pepper
    mixed vegetables, to serve

COOK'S TIP
To serve this dish for a dinner party, rather than serve it in a large dish, once it has cooked, stamp out rounds using a 5cm/2in cutter and serve on a bed of salad leaves.

1 Preheat the oven to 180°C/350°F/ Gas 4. Cook the potatoes in a large saucepan of lightly salted boiling water for 15 minutes until they are just tender. Drain and leave to cool slightly. When cool enough to handle cut the potatoes into even 3mm/⅛in slices.

2 Grease the base and sides of a 1.2 litre/2 pint/5 cup casserole dish. Lay a few potato slices over the base of the dish. Scatter a few shallots over and season well.

3 Drain the oil from the mussels into a bowl. Slice the mussels and add them again to the reserved oil. Stir in the chives and soured cream with half of the cheese. Spoon a little of the sauce over the layer of potatoes.

4 Continue to layer the potatoes, shallots and the sauce. Finish with a layer of potatoes and sprinkle over the remainder of the cheese.

5 Bake for 30–45 minutes. Remove from the oven and serve while hot with a selection of mixed vegetables.

JANSSON'S TEMPTATION

THIS IS ONE OF SWEDEN'S MOST FAMOUS DISHES. LAYERED WITH ANCHOVIES AND ONIONS AND BAKED WITH CREAM, THE POTATOES TAKE ON A WONDERFUL FLAVOUR.

SERVES SIX

INGREDIENTS
    1kg/2¼lb potatoes
    2 very large onions
    2–3 tins anchovy fillets
    ground black pepper
    150ml/¼ pint/⅔ cup single cream
    25g/1oz/2 tbsp butter, finely diced,
       plus extra for greasing
    150ml/¼ pint/⅔ cup double cream

COOK'S TIP
To make this recipe in individual
portions, pile all the ingredients except
for the double cream on to large squares
of buttered foil. Gather up the edges
and bring them together. Bake for
40 minutes, then complete according
to the recipe.

1 Preheat the oven to 220°C/425°F/
Gas 7. Peel the potatoes and cut into
matchsticks. Slice the onions into rings.

2 Grease a 1.75 litre/3 pint/7½ cup
casserole dish. Layer half the potatoes
and onions in it. Drain the anchovies
into a bowl, reserving the oil and lay the
fillets over the potatoes, then layer the
remaining potatoes and onions. Season.

3 Mix the anchovy oil and single cream
together. Then pour evenly over the
potatoes. Dot the surface with butter.

4 Cover the potatoes with foil and
tightly seal the edges. Bake for 1 hour
in the oven. Remove from the oven,
taste and adjust the seasonings if
necessary. Pour the double cream over
and serve immediately.

INDONESIAN PRAWNS
WITH SLICED POTATOES

WITH A FRESH TASTING COMBINATION OF PRAWNS AND THINLY SLICED POTATOES MADE IN INDONESIAN STYLE WITH SATAY SAUCE, THIS DISH IS SURPRISINGLY RICH AND FILLING.

SERVES FOUR

INGREDIENTS
    2 large waxy maincrop potatoes,
       peeled and cut in half
    120ml/4fl oz/½ cup vegetable oil
    1 bunch spring onions, finely sliced
    2 red chillies, seeded and diced
    450g/1lb peeled cooked prawns
    45ml/3 tbsp crunchy peanut butter
    200ml/7fl oz/⅞ cup coconut cream
    15ml/1 tbsp dark soy sauce
    1 bunch chopped fresh coriander
    salt

COOK'S TIP
For a more luxurious version, replace the
cooked, peeled prawns with fresh raw,
shelled king prawns.

1 Cook the potatoes in lightly salted
boiling water for 15 minutes until
tender. Drain and when cool enough to
handle cut into 3mm/⅛in slices. Heat
the oil in a frying pan and sauté the
potatoes for 10 minutes, turning
occasionally until browned. Drain on
kitchen paper and keep hot.

2 Drain off almost all of the oil from the
pan and fry the spring onions and half
the chillies in the pan for 1 minute. Add
the prawns and toss for a few seconds.

3 Beat together the peanut butter,
coconut cream, soy sauce and
remaining chilli. Add this sauce to the
prawns and cook for a further minute or
two until thoroughly heated through.

4 Lightly grease a large oval platter
and arrange the prepared potatoes
evenly around the base. Spoon the
prawn mixture over until the potatoes
are mostly covered over. Top with
the coriander.

CLASSIC FISH AND CHIPS

NOTHING BEATS A PIECE OF COD COOKED TO A CRISP WITH FRESHLY MADE CHIPS ON THE SIDE. THE BATTER SHOULD BE LIGHT AND CRISP, BUT NOT TOO GREASY AND THE FISH SHOULD MELT IN THE MOUTH. SERVE WITH LIME WEDGES IF YOU REALLY WANT TO TART IT UP. THE SECRETS OF COOKING FISH AND CHIPS SUCCESSFULLY ARE TO MAKE SURE THE OIL IS FRESH AND CLEAN. HEAT THE OIL TO THE CORRECT TEMPERATURE BEFORE COOKING THE CHIPS AND AGAIN BEFORE ADDING THE FISH. SERVE THE DISH IMMEDIATELY, WHILE STILL CRISP AND PIPING HOT.

SERVES FOUR

INGREDIENTS
   450g/1lb potatoes
   groundnut oil for deep fat frying
   4 x 175g/6oz cod fillets, skinned
   and any tiny bones removed
For the batter
   75g/3oz/⅔ cup plain flour
   1 egg yolk
   10ml/2 tsp oil
   salt
   lemon wedges, to garnish

1 Cut the potatoes into 5mm/¼in thick slices. Cut each slice again to make 5mm/¼in chips.

2 Heat the oil in a deep fat fryer to 180°C/350°F. Add the chips to the fryer and cook for 3 minutes, then remove from the pan and shake off all fat. Set to one side.

3 To make the batter, sift the flour into a bowl and add the remaining ingredients with a pinch of salt. Beat well until smooth. Set aside until ready to use.

4 Cook the chips again in the fat for a further 5 minutes or so until they are really nice and crisp. Drain on kitchen paper and season with salt. Keep hot in a low oven while you cook the pieces of fish.

VARIATION
Although cod is the traditional choice for fish and chips, you can also use haddock. Rock salmon, sometimes sold as huss or dogfish, also has a good flavour. It has a central bone which cannot be removed before cooking otherwise the pieces of fish will fall apart, but can be easily prized out once the fish is served.

5 Dip the fish into the batter, making sure they are evenly coated and shake off any excess.

6 Carefully lower the fish into the fat and cook for 5 minutes. Drain on kitchen paper. Serve with lemon wedges and the chips.

COOK'S TIP
Use fresh rather than frozen fish for the very best texture and flavour. If you have to use frozen fish, defrost it thoroughly and make sure it is dry before coating with batter.

CARIBBEAN CRAB CAKES

CRAB MEAT MAKES WONDERFUL FISH CAKES, AS EVIDENCED WITH THESE GUTSY MORSELS. SERVED WITH A RICH TOMATO DIP, THEY BECOME GREAT PARTY FOOD TOO, ON "STICKS".

MAKES ABOUT FIFTEEN

INGREDIENTS
    225g/8oz white crab meat (fresh,
      frozen or canned)
    115g/4oz cooked floury potatoes,
      mashed
    30ml/2 tbsp fresh herb seasoning
    2.5ml/½ tsp mild mustard
    2.5ml/½ tsp ground black pepper
    ½ fresh hot chilli pepper,
      finely chopped
    5ml/1 tsp fresh oregano
    1 egg, beaten
    plain flour, for dredging
    vegetable oil, for frying
    lime wedges and coriander sprigs,
      to garnish
    fresh whole chilli peppers, to garnish
For the tomato dip
    15g/½oz/1 tbsp butter or margarine
    ½ onion, finely chopped
    2 canned plum tomatoes, chopped
    1 garlic clove, crushed
    150ml/¼ pint/⅔ cup water
    5–10ml/1–2 tsp malt vinegar
    15ml/1 tbsp chopped fresh coriander
    ½ hot fresh chilli pepper, chopped

1 To make the crab cakes, mix together the crab meat, potatoes, herb seasoning, mustard, peppers, oregano and egg in a large bowl. Chill the mixture in the bowl for at least 30 minutes.

2 Meanwhile, make the tomato dip to accompany the crab cakes. Melt the butter or margarine in a small pan over a medium heat.

3 Add the onion, tomatoes and garlic and sauté for about 5 minutes until the onion is tender. Add the water, vinegar, coriander and hot chilli pepper. Bring to the boil then reduce the heat and simmer for 10 minutes.

4 Transfer the mixture to a food processor or blender and blend to a smooth purée. Pour into a bowl. Keep warm or chill as wished.

5 Using a spoon, shape the crab into rounds and dredge with flour, shaking off the excess. Heat a little oil in a frying pan and fry, a few at a time, for 2–3 minutes on each side. Drain on kitchen paper and keep warm in a low oven while cooking the remainder.

6 Serve with the tomato dip and garnish with lime wedges, coriander sprigs and whole chillies.

PILCHARD <u>AND</u> LEEK POTATO CAKES

THIS IS A SIMPLE SUPPER USING A SELECTION OF BASIC STORE CUPBOARD INGREDIENTS. USING PILCHARDS IN TOMATO SAUCE GIVES A GREATER DEPTH OF FLAVOUR TO THE FINISHED DISH.

SERVES SIX

INGREDIENTS
225g/8oz potatoes, diced
425g/15oz can pilchards in tomato
  sauce, boned and flaked
1 small leek, very finely diced
5ml/1 tsp lemon juice
salt and ground black pepper
For the coating
1 egg, beaten
75g/3oz/1½ cups fresh white
  breadcrumbs
vegetable oil for frying
salad leaves, cucumber and lemon
  wedges, to garnish
mayonnaise, to serve

1 Cook the potatoes in lightly salted boiling water for 10 minutes or until tender. Drain, mash, and cool.

2 Add the pilchards and their tomato sauce, leeks and lemon juice. Season with salt and pepper and then beat well until you have formed a smooth paste. Chill for 30 minutes.

3 Divide the mixture into six pieces and shape into cakes. Dip each cake in the egg and then the breadcrumbs.

4 Heat the oil and shallow fry the fish cakes on each side for 5 minutes. Drain on kitchen paper and garnish with salad leaves, cucumber ribbons and lemon wedges. Serve with mayonnaise.

TUNA AND CORN FISH CAKES

DEFINITELY ONE FOR YOUNGER MEMBERS OF THE FAMILY WHO LIKE THE SWEET TASTE OF CORN.
THEY MAY EVEN HELP YOU MAKE SOME FISHY-SHAPED CAKES.

SERVES FOUR

INGREDIENTS
   300g/11oz mashed potatoes
   200g/7oz can tuna fish in
     soya oil, drained
   115g/4oz/¾ cup canned or frozen
     sweetcorn
   30ml/2 tbsp chopped fresh parsley
   50g/2oz/1 cup fresh white or brown
     breadcrumbs
   salt and ground black pepper
   grilled baby plum tomatoes and
     salad potatoes, to serve

VARIATIONS
For simple storecupboard variations,
try using canned sardines, red or pink
salmon, or smoked mackerel in place of
the tuna and instant mash when you're
in a real hurry!

1 Preheat the grill. Place the mashed
potatoes in a large bowl and stir in the
tuna fish, sweetcorn and chopped
fresh parsley.

2 Season the mixture to taste with salt
and pepper and mix together
thoroughly, then shape into eight
patty shapes.

3 Lightly coat the fish cakes in the
breadcrumbs, pressing to adhere, then
place on a baking sheet.

4 Cook the fish cakes under the hot
grill until crisp and golden brown on
both sides, turning once. Serve hot with
grilled baby plum tomatoes and small
salad potatoes.

SWEET POTATO, PUMPKIN AND PRAWN CAKES

THIS UNUSUAL ASIAN COMBINATION MAKES A DELICIOUS DISH WHICH NEEDS ONLY A FISH SAUCE OR
SOY SAUCE TO DIP INTO. SERVE WITH NOODLES OR FRIED RICE FOR A LIGHT MEAL.

SERVES FOUR

INGREDIENTS
   200g/7oz/1⅔ cups strong white
     bread flour
   2.5ml/½ tsp salt
   2.5ml/½ tsp dried yeast
   175ml/6fl oz/¾ cup warm water
   1 egg, beaten
   200g/7oz fresh prawn tails, peeled
   225g/8oz pumpkin, peeled, seeded
     and grated
   150g/5oz sweet potato, grated
   2 spring onions, chopped
   50g/2oz water chestnuts, chopped
   2.5ml/½ tsp chilli sauce
   1 garlic clove, crushed
   juice of ½ lime
   vegetable oil, for deep-frying
   lime wedges, to serve

1 Sift together the flour and salt into a
large bowl and make a well in the
centre. In a separate container dissolve
the yeast in the water until creamy then
pour into the centre of the flour and salt
mixture. Pour in the egg and set aside
for a few minutes until bubbles appear.
Mix to form a smooth batter.

2 Place the prawns in a saucepan
with just enough water to cover. Bring
to the boil then reduce the heat and
simmer for about 10 minutes. Drain,
rinse in cold water and drain again
well. Roughly chop then place in a
bowl along with the pumpkin and
sweet potato.

3 Add the spring onions, water
chestnuts, chilli sauce, garlic and lime
juice and mix well. Fold into the batter
mixture carefully until evenly mixed.

4 Heat a 1cm/½in layer of oil in a large
frying pan until really hot. Spoon in the
batter in heaps, leaving space between
each one, and fry until golden on both
sides. Drain on kitchen paper and serve
with the lime wedges.

Vegetarian Dishes

POTATOES ARE USED IMAGINATIVELY IN
MANY VEGETARIAN DISHES. USE THEM TO
TOP A PIZZA, ADD TO A RICH CHEESY BAKE
OR TRY THEM IN A SPICY POTATO STRUDEL.
MANY COUNTRIES HAVE THEIR OWN
SIGNATURE DISHES, SUCH AS ITALIAN
GNOCCHI OR GREEK TOMATO AND
POTATO BAKE, WHERE CHUNKS OF
POTATO ARE SLOW COOKED WITH
MEDITERRANEAN RIPENED
TOMATOES AND GARLIC —
SIMPLY DELICIOUS.

CHINESE POTATOES WITH CHILLI BEANS

EAST MEETS WEST IN THIS AMERICAN-STYLE DISH WITH A CHINESE FLAVOUR — THE SAUCE IS PARTICULARLY TASTY. TRY IT AS A QUICK SUPPER WHEN YOU FANCY A MEAL WITH A LITTLE ZING!

SERVES FOUR

INGREDIENTS
    4 medium firm or waxy potatoes,
        cut into thick chunks
    30ml/2 tbsp sunflower or
        groundnut oil
    3 spring onions, sliced
    1 large fresh chilli, seeded and sliced
    2 garlic cloves, crushed
    400g/14oz can red kidney
        beans, drained
    30ml/2 tbsp soy sauce
    15ml/1 tbsp sesame oil
    15ml/1 tbsp sesame seeds,
        to garnish
    chopped fresh coriander or parsley,
        to garnish
    salt and ground black pepper

1 Cook the potatoes in boiling water until they are just tender. Take care not to overcook them. Drain and reserve.

2 Heat the oil in a large frying pan or wok over a medium-high heat. Add the spring onions and chilli and stir-fry for about 1 minute, then add the garlic and stir-fry for a few seconds longer.

3 Add the potatoes, stirring well, then the beans and finally the soy sauce and sesame oil.

4 Season to taste and continue to cook the vegetables until they are well heated through. Sprinkle with the sesame seeds and the coriander or parsley and serve hot.

GREEK TOMATO AND POTATO BAKE

AN ADAPTATION OF A CLASSIC GREEK DISH, WHICH IS USUALLY COOKED ON THE HOB. THIS RECIPE HAS A RICHER FLAVOUR AS IT IS STOVE COOKED FIRST AND THEN BAKED IN THE OVEN.

SERVES FOUR

INGREDIENTS
    120ml/4fl oz/½ cup olive oil
    1 large onion, finely chopped
    3 garlic cloves, crushed
    4 large ripe tomatoes, peeled,
        deseeded and chopped
    1kg/2¼lb even-size main crop
        waxy potatoes
    salt and freshly ground black pepper
    flat leaf parsley, to garnish

COOK'S TIP
Make sure that the potatoes are completely coated in the oil for even cooking.

1 Preheat the oven to 180°C/350°F/ Gas 4. Heat the oil in a flameproof casserole. Fry the onion and garlic for 5 minutes until softened and just starting to brown.

2 Add the tomatoes to the pan, season and cook for 1 minute. Cut the potatoes into wedges. Add to the pan. Cook for 10 minutes. Season again and cover with a tight fitting lid.

3 Place the covered casserole on the middle shelf of the oven and cook for 45 minutes–1 hour. Garnish with flat leaf parsley.

POTATO AND CABBAGE RISSOLES

ORIGINALLY MADE ON MONDAYS WITH LEFTOVER POTATOES AND CABBAGE FROM THE SUNDAY LUNCH, THESE RISSOLES ARE QUICK TO MAKE AND GREAT FOR ANY LIGHT MEAL. OR MAKE THEM FOR BRUNCH TEAMED WITH FRIED EGGS, GRILLED TOMATOES AND MUSHROOMS.

SERVES FOUR

INGREDIENTS
   450g/1lb mashed potato
   225g/8oz steamed or boiled cabbage
     or kale, shredded
   1 egg, beaten
   115g/4oz/1 cup Cheddar cheese,
     grated
   freshly grated nutmeg
   plain flour, for coating
   vegetable oil, for frying
   salt and ground black pepper
   lettuce, to serve

COOK'S TIP
If you want to flavour the rissoles with a stronger tasting cheese, try a blue, such as Stilton or Shropshire Blue.

1 Mix the potato with the cabbage or kale, egg, cheese, nutmeg and seasoning. Divide and shape into eight small sausage shapes.

2 Chill for an hour or so, if possible, as this enables the rissoles to become firm and makes them easier to fry. Dredge them in the flour, shaking off the excess.

3 Heat a 1cm/½in layer of oil in a frying pan until it is really hot. Carefully slide the rissoles into the oil and fry in batches on each side for about 3 minutes until golden and crisp.

4 Remove the rissoles from the pan and drain on kitchen paper. Serve piping hot with fresh lettuce leaves.

POTATO, MOZZARELLA AND GARLIC PIZZA

NEW POTATOES, SMOKED MOZZARELLA AND GARLIC MAKE THIS PIZZA UNIQUE. YOU COULD ADD SLICED SMOKED PORK SAUSAGE OR PASTRAMI TO MAKE IT EVEN MORE SUBSTANTIAL.

SERVES TWO TO THREE

INGREDIENTS
   350g/12oz small new or
     salad potatoes
   45ml/3 tbsp olive oil
   2 garlic cloves, crushed
   1 pizza base, 25–30cm/
     10–12 in diameter
   1 red onion, thinly sliced
   150g/5oz/1¼ cups smoked mozzarella
     cheese, grated
   10ml/2 tsp chopped fresh rosemary
     or sage
   salt and ground black pepper
   30ml/2 tbsp freshly grated Parmesan
     cheese, to garnish

1 Preheat the oven to 220°C/425°F/ Gas 7. Cook the potatoes in boiling salted water for 5 minutes. Drain well and leave to cool. Peel and slice thinly.

2 Heat 30ml/2 tbsp of the oil in a frying pan. Add the sliced potatoes and garlic and fry for 5–8 minutes turning frequently until tender.

3 Brush the pizza base with the remaining oil. Scatter the onion over, then arrange the potatoes on top.

4 Sprinkle over the mozzarella and rosemary or sage and plenty of black pepper. Bake for 15–20 minutes until golden. Remove from the oven, sprinkle with Parmesan and more black pepper.

PUMPKIN GNOCCHI <u>WITH A</u> CHANTERELLE PARSLEY CREAM

ITALIANS LOVE PUMPKIN AND OFTEN INCORPORATE IT INTO THEIR DUMPLINGS AND OTHER TRADITIONAL PASTA DISHES AS IT ADDS A SLIGHT SWEET RICHNESS. THESE GNOCCHI ARE SUPERB ON THEIR OWN BUT THEY ARE ALSO GREAT SERVED WITH MEAT OR GAME.

SERVES FOUR

INGREDIENTS
450g/1lb floury potatoes
450g/1lb pumpkin, peeled, seeded
   and chopped
2 egg yolks
200g/7oz/1¾ cups plain flour, plus
   more if necessary
pinch of ground allspice
1.5ml/¼ tsp cinnamon
pinch of freshly grated nutmeg
finely grated rind of ½ orange
salt and ground pepper
For the sauce
30ml/2 tbsp olive oil
1 shallot, finely chopped
175g/6oz/2½ cups fresh chanterelles,
   sliced, or 15g/½oz/½ cup dried,
   soaked in warm water for
   20 minutes, then drained
10ml/2 tsp almond butter
150ml/¼ pint/⅔ cup crème fraîche
a little milk or water
75ml/5 tbsp chopped fresh parsley
50g/2oz/½ cup Parmesan cheese,
   freshly grated

1 Cook the potatoes in a large saucepan of boiling salted water for 20 minutes. Drain and set aside.

2 Place the pumpkin in a bowl, cover and microwave on full power for 8 minutes. Alternatively, wrap the pumpkin in foil and bake at 180°C/350°F/Gas 4 for 30 minutes. Drain well.

3 Pass the pumpkin and potatoes through a food mill into a bowl. Add the egg yolks, flour, spices, orange rind and seasoning and mix well to make a soft dough. If you find that the mixture is too loose you can add a little more flour to stiffen it up.

4 Bring a large pan of salted water to a fast boil. Meanwhile, spread a layer of flour on a clean work surface. Spoon the prepared gnocchi mixture into a piping bag fitted with a 1cm/½in plain nozzle.

VARIATION
Turn these gnocchi into a main meal for vegetarians by serving them with a rich home-made tomato sauce. If you want to make the dish more special, serve the gnocchi with a side dish of ratatouille made from courgettes, peppers and aubergines, cooked gently with tomatoes, plenty of garlic and really good extra virgin olive oil.

5 Pipe directly on to the flour to make a 15cm/6in sausage. Roll in flour and cut crossways into 2.5cm/1in pieces. Repeat to make more sausage shapes and pieces. Mark each lightly with the tines of a fork and drop into the boiling water. When they rise to the surface, after 3–4 minutes, they are done.

6 Meanwhile make the sauce. Heat the oil in a non-stick frying pan, add the shallot and fry until soft but not coloured. Add the chanterelles and cook briefly, then add the almond butter. Stir to melt and stir in the crème fraîche. Simmer briefly and adjust the consistency with milk or water. Add the parsley and season to taste.

7 Lift the gnocchi out of the water with a slotted spoon, drain well, and turn into bowls. Spoon the sauce over the top, sprinkle with grated Parmesan, and serve at once.

COOK'S TIPS
If planning ahead, gnocchi can be shaped, ready for cooking, up to 8 hours in advance. Almond butter is available from health food shops.

TRUFFADE

BAKED UNTIL MELTINGLY SOFT, THIS WARMING CHEESE AND POTATO SUPPER IS THE PERFECT SLOW BAKE TO COME HOME TO. IN FRANCE, WHERE IT ORIGINATED, IT WOULD BE MADE WITH A TOMME OR CANTAL CHEESE WHICH ARE NOW READILY AVAILABLE.

SERVES FOUR TO SIX

INGREDIENTS
   a little sunflower oil or melted butter
   1 large onion, thinly sliced
   675g/1½lb baking potatoes, very
      thinly sliced
   150g/5oz/1¼ cups grated hard
      cheese, such as Tomme, Cantal or
      mature Cheddar
   freshly grated nutmeg
   salt and ground black pepper
   mixed salad leaves, to serve

VARIATION
In France, they make a non-vegetarian
version of this dish, which is cooked with
diced streaky bacon (lardons) and the
cheese is chopped, not grated. The
ingredients are mixed and cooked
slowly in a little lard in a pan on top
of the stove.

1 Preheat the oven to 180°C/350°F/
Gas 4. Lightly grease the base of a
shallow baking dish or roasting tin with
the oil or melted butter.

2 Arrange a layer of onions over the
bottom of the dish and then add a
layer of potatoes over them, and a
sprinkling of cheese. Finish with a layer
of potatoes.

3 Brush the top layer of potatoes with
oil or melted butter and season with
nutmeg, salt and pepper.

4 Top the dish with a layer of cheese.
Bake for 1 hour 5 minutes until the
vegetables are tender and the top is
golden brown. Leave the dish to stand
for about 5 minutes, then serve in
wedges with a salad.

POTATOES BAKED WITH TOMATOES

THIS SIMPLE, HEARTY DISH FROM THE SOUTH OF ITALY IS BEST WHEN TOMATOES ARE IN SEASON AND BURSTING WITH FLAVOUR, BUT IT CAN ALSO BE MADE WITH CANNED PLUM TOMATOES.

SERVES SIX

INGREDIENTS
   2 large red or yellow onions,
      thinly sliced
   1kg/2¼lb baking potatoes,
      thinly sliced
   450g/1lb tomatoes, fresh or canned,
      sliced, with their juice
   90ml/6 tbsp olive oil
   115g/4oz/1 cup Parmesan
      or Cheddar cheese,
      freshly grated
   a few fresh basil leaves
   50ml/2fl oz/¼ cup water
   salt and ground black pepper

1 Preheat the oven to 180°C/350°F/
Gas 4. Brush a large baking dish
generously with oil.

2 Arrange a layer of some onions in
the base of the dish, followed by layers
of some potatoes and tomatoes
alternating them to make the dish look
colourful. Pour a little of the oil over the
surface, and sprinkle with some of the
cheese. Season with salt and ground
black pepper.

3 Continue to layer the vegetables in
the dish until they are used up, ending
with an overlapping layer of potatoes
and tomatoes. Tear the basil leaves into
small pieces, and add them here and
there among the vegetables, saving a
few for garnish. Sprinkle the top with
the remaining grated cheese and oil.

4 Pour the water over the dish. Bake in
the oven for 1 hour until the vegetables
are tender.

5 Check the potato dish towards the
end of cooking and if the top begins to
brown too much, place a sheet of foil or
greaseproof paper, or a flat baking tray
on top of the dish. Garnish the dish with
the remaining fresh basil, once it is
cooked, and serve hot.

LAYERED VEGETABLE TERRINE

*A COMBINATION OF VEGETABLES AND HERBS LAYERED AND BAKED IN A SPINACH-LINED LOAF TIN.
DELICIOUS SERVED HOT OR WARM WITH A SIMPLE SALAD GARNISH.*

SERVES SIX

INGREDIENTS
3 red peppers, halved
450g/1lb main crop waxy potatoes
115g/4oz spinach leaves, trimmed
25g/1oz/2 tbsp butter
pinch grated nutmeg
115g/4oz/1 cup vegetarian Cheddar
    cheese, grated
1 medium courgette, sliced
    lengthways and blanched
salt and ground black pepper

1 Preheat the oven to 180°C/350°F/
Gas 4. Place the peppers in a roasting
tin and roast, cores in place, for 30–45
minutes until charred. Remove from the
oven. Place in a plastic bag to cool.
Peel the skins and remove the cores.
Halve the potatoes and boil in lightly
salted water for 10–15 minutes.

2 Blanch the spinach for a few
seconds in boiling water. Drain and pat
dry on kitchen paper. Line the base and
sides of a 900g/2lb loaf tin, making sure
the leaves overlap slightly.

3 Slice the potatoes thinly and lay one-
third of the potatoes over the base, dot
with a little of the butter and season
with salt, pepper and nutmeg. Sprinkle
a little cheese over.

4 Arrange 3 of the peeled pepper
halves on top. Sprinkle a little cheese
over and then a layer of courgettes. Lay
another one-third of the potatoes on top
with the remaining peppers and some
more cheese, seasoning as you go. Lay
the final layer of potato on top and
scatter over any remaining cheese. Fold
the spinach leaves over. Cover with foil.

5 Place the loaf tin in a roasting tin
and pour boiling water around the
outside, making sure the water comes
halfway up the sides of the tin. Bake for
45 minutes–1 hour. Remove from the
oven and turn the loaf out. Serve sliced
with lettuce and tomatoes.

ALOO SAAG

TRADITIONAL INDIAN SPICES — MUSTARD SEED, GINGER AND CHILLI — GIVE A REALLY GOOD KICK TO POTATOES AND SPINACH IN THIS DELICIOUS AND AUTHENTIC CURRY.

SERVES TWO

INGREDIENTS
    450g/1lb spinach
    30ml/2 tbsp vegetable oil
    5ml/1 tsp black mustard seeds
    1 onion, thinly sliced
    2 garlic cloves, crushed
    2.5cm/1in piece root ginger,
      finely chopped
    675g/1½lb firm potatoes, cut into
      2.5cm/1in chunks
    5ml/1 tsp chilli powder
    5ml/1 tsp salt
    120ml/4fl oz/½ cup water

COOK'S TIPS
To make certain that the spinach is dry, put it in a clean tea towel, roll up tightly and squeeze gently to remove any excess liquid. Choose a firm waxy variety of potato or a salad potato so the pieces do not break up during cooking.

1 Blanch the spinach in boiling water for 3–4 minutes.

2 Drain the spinach thoroughly and leave to cool. When it is cool enough to handle, use your hands to squeeze out any remaining liquid.

3 Heat the oil in a large saucepan and fry the mustard seeds for 2 minutes, stirring, until they begin to splutter.

4 Add the onion, garlic and ginger and fry for 5 minutes, stirring.

5 Stir in the potatoes, chilli powder, salt and water and cook for 8 minutes, stirring occasionally.

6 Finally, add the spinach to the pan. Cover and simmer for 10–15 minutes until the spinach is cooked and the potatoes are tender. Serve hot.

POTATO CAKES WITH GOAT'S CHEESE

GRILLED GOAT'S CHEESE MAKES A DELICATELY TANGY AND GENTLY BUBBLING TOPPING FOR THESE HERBY POTATO CAKES. SERVE WITH A FLAVOURSOME SALAD.

SERVES TWO TO FOUR

INGREDIENTS
   450g/1lb floury potatoes
   10ml/2 tsp chopped fresh thyme
   1 garlic clove, crushed
   2 spring onions (including the green
      parts), finely chopped
   30ml/2 tbsp olive oil
   50g/2oz/4 tbsp unsalted butter
   2 x 65g/2½oz firm goat's cheese
   salt and ground black pepper
   salad leaves, such as curly endive,
      radicchio and lamb's lettuce, tossed
      in walnut dressing, to serve
   thyme sprigs, to garnish

COOK'S TIP
These potato cakes make great party
snacks. Make them half the size and
serve warm on a large platter.

1 Coarsely grate the potatoes. Using
your hands, squeeze out as much of
the thick starchy liquid as possible,
then gently combine with the chopped
thyme, garlic, spring onions and
seasoning.

2 Heat half the oil and butter in a non-
stick frying pan. Add two large
spoonfuls of the potato mixture, spacing
them well apart, and press firmly down
with a spatula. Cook for 3–4 minutes on
each side until golden.

3 Drain the potato cakes on kitchen
paper and keep warm in a low oven.
Heat the remaining oil and butter and
fry two more potato cakes in the same
way with the remaining mixture.
Meanwhile preheat the grill.

4 Cut the cheese in half horizontally
and place one half, cut side up, on
each potato cake. Grill for 2–3 minutes
until lightly golden. Serve on plates and
arrange the salad leaves around them.
Garnish with thyme sprigs.

WILD MUSHROOM GRATIN WITH BEAUFORT CHEESE, NEW POTATOES AND WALNUTS

THIS IS ONE OF THE SIMPLEST AND MOST DELICIOUS WAYS OF COOKING MUSHROOMS. SERVE THIS DISH AS THE SWISS DO, WITH NEW POTATOES AND GHERKINS.

SERVES FOUR

INGREDIENTS
   900g/2lb small new or
      salad potatoes
   50g/2oz/4 tbsp unsalted butter or
      60ml/4 tbsp olive oil
   350g/12oz/5 cups assorted wild and
      cultivated mushrooms, thinly sliced
   175g/6oz Beaufort or Fontina cheese,
      thinly sliced
   50g/2oz/½ cup broken walnuts,
      toasted
   salt and ground black pepper
   12 gherkins and mixed green salad
      leaves, to serve

1 Cook the potatoes in boiling salted
water for 20 minutes until tender. Drain
and return to the pan. Add a knob of
butter or oil and cover to keep warm.

2 Heat the remaining butter or the oil
in a frying pan over a medium-high
heat. Add the mushrooms and fry until
their juices appear, then increase the
heat and fry until most of their juices
have cooked away. Season.

3 Meanwhile preheat the grill. Arrange
the cheese on top of the mushroom
slices, place the pan under the grill and
grill until bubbly and golden brown.
Scatter the gratin with walnuts and
serve at once with the buttered
potatoes and sliced gherkins. Serve a
side dish of mixed green salad to
complete this meal.

SPICY POTATO STRUDEL

WRAP UP A TASTY MIXTURE OF VEGETABLES IN A SPICY, CREAMY SAUCE WITH CRISP FILO PASTRY.
SERVE WITH A GOOD SELECTION OF CHUTNEYS OR A YOGURT SAUCE.

SERVES FOUR

INGREDIENTS
1 onion, chopped
2 carrots, coarsely grated
1 courgette, chopped
350g/12oz firm potatoes,
   finely chopped
65g/2½oz/5 tbsp butter
10ml/2 tsp mild curry paste
2.5ml/½ tsp dried thyme
150ml/¼ pint/⅔ cup water
1 egg, beaten
30ml/2 tbsp single cream
50g/2oz/½ cup Cheddar
   cheese, grated
8 sheets filo pastry, thawed if frozen
sesame seeds, for sprinkling
salt and ground black pepper

1 In a large frying pan cook the onion, carrots, courgette and potatoes in 25g/1oz/2 tbsp of the butter for 5 minutes tossing frequently so they cook evenly. Add the curry paste and stir in. Continue to cook, the vegetables for a further minute or so.

2 Add the thyme, water and seasoning. Bring to the boil then reduce the heat and simmer for 10 minutes until tender, stirring occasionally.

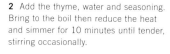

3 Remove from the heat and leave to cool. Transfer the mixture into a large bowl and then mix in the egg, cream and cheese. Chill until ready to fill the filo pastry.

4 Melt the remaining butter and lay out four sheets of filo pastry, slightly overlapping them to form a fairly large rectangle. Brush with some melted butter and fit the other sheets on top. Brush again.

5 Preheat the oven to 190°C/375°F/ Gas 5. Spoon the filling along one long side, then roll up the pastry. Form it into a circle and set on a baking sheet. Brush again with the last of the butter and sprinkle over the sesame seeds.

6 Bake the strudel in the oven for about 25 minutes until golden and crisp. Stand for 5 minutes before cutting.

PEPPER AND POTATO TORTILLA

TORTILLA IS TRADITIONALLY A SPANISH DISH LIKE A THICK OMELETTE, BEST EATEN COLD IN CHUNKY WEDGES. IT MAKES IDEAL PICNICKING FOOD. USE A HARD SPANISH CHEESE, LIKE MAHÓN, OR A GOAT'S CHEESE, ALTHOUGH SHARP CHEDDAR MAKES A GOOD SUBSTITUTE.

SERVES FOUR

INGREDIENTS
    2 medium firm potatoes
    45ml/3 tbsp olive oil, plus more
      if necessary
    1 large onion, thinly sliced
    2 garlic cloves, crushed
    2 peppers, one green and one red,
      seeded and thinly sliced
    6 eggs, beaten
    115g/4oz/1 cup sharp cheese, grated
    salt and ground black pepper

VARIATION
You can add any sliced and lightly cooked vegetable, such as mushrooms, courgette or broccoli, to this tortilla instead of the green and red peppers. Cooked pasta or brown rice are both excellent alternatives to the potatoes.

1 Par-boil the potatoes in boiling water for about 10 minutes. Drain and leave to cool slightly. Slice them thickly. Preheat the grill.

2 In a large non-stick or well-seasoned frying pan, heat the oil over a medium heat. Add the onion, garlic and peppers and cook for 5 minutes until softened.

3 Add the potatoes and continue frying, stirring occasionally, until the potatoes are tender.

4 Pour in half the beaten eggs, sprinkle half the cheese over this and then the remainder of the egg. Season. Finish with a layer of cheese. Reduce the heat to low and continue to cook without stirring, half covering the pan with a lid to help set the eggs.

5 When the tortilla is firm, place the pan under the hot grill to seal the top just lightly. Leave the tortilla in the pan to cool. Serve at room temperature, cut into wedges.

Breads and Scones

POTATOES PLAY AN ESSENTIAL PART IN MANY LOCAL
AND REGIONAL BREAD AND SCONE
DISHES. TRY RUSSIAN POTATO
BREAD, KARTOFFELBROT OR
HERB POTATO SCONES AND BE
SURPRISED AT THEIR LIGHT
TEXTURE AND WONDERFUL
FLAVOUR. INDULGE YOURSELF WITH
AN UNUSUAL RICH CHOCOLATE
POTATO CAKE. THE ADDITION OF
POTATO MAKES THE CAKE DELICIOUSLY
MOIST AND IT'S SURE TO BE AN
INSTANT SUCCESS.

SWEET POTATO BREAD WITH CINNAMON AND WALNUTS

A WONDERFUL BRUNCH DISH, AND COMPLETELY DELICIOUS SERVED WITH CRISPY BACON.

3 Drain the potatoes and cool in cold water, then peel the skins. Mash the potatoes with a fork and mix into the dry ingredients with the nuts.

4 Make a well in the centre and pour in the milk. Bring the mixture together with a round-bladed knife, place on to a floured surface and knead for 5 minutes.

MAKES A 900G/2LB LOAF

INGREDIENTS
   1 medium sweet potato
   5ml/1 tsp ground cinnamon
   450g/1lb/4 cups strong white flour
   5ml/1 tsp easy-blend dried yeast
   50g/2oz/½ cup walnut pieces
   300ml/½ pint/1¼ cups warmed milk
   salt and ground black pepper
   oil, for greasing

COOK'S TIP
For an extra-crispy loaf, after the bread is cooked, remove from the tin and return the bread to the oven placing it upside down on the oven rack. Continue to cook for a further 5 minutes.

1 Boil the whole potato in its skin for 45 minutes or until tender.

2 Meanwhile, sift the cinnamon and flour together into a large bowl. Stir in the dried yeast.

5 Return the dough to a bowl and cover with a damp cloth. Leave to rise for 1 hour or until doubled in size. Turn the dough out and knock back to remove any air bubbles. Knead again for a few minutes. If the dough feels sticky add more flour to the mixture. Shape into a ball and place the bread in an oiled and base-lined 900g/2lb loaf tin. Cover with a damp cloth and leave to rise in a warm place for 1 hour or until doubled in size.

6 Preheat the oven to 200°C/400°F/ Gas 6. Bake on the middle shelf of the oven for 25 minutes. Turn out and tap the base; if it sounds hollow the bread is cooked. Cool on a wire rack.

THREE HERB POTATO SCONES

THESE FLAVOURSOME SCONES ARE PERFECT SERVED WARM AND SPLIT IN TWO WITH HAND-CARVED HAM AND PARMESAN SHAVINGS AS A FILLING.

MAKES TWELVE

INGREDIENTS
225g/8oz/2 cups self-raising flour
5ml/1 tsp baking powder
pinch of salt
50g/2oz/4 tbsp butter, diced
25g/1oz potato flakes
15ml/1 tbsp chopped fresh parsley
15ml/1 tbsp chopped fresh basil
15ml/1 tbsp chopped fresh oregano
150ml/¼ pint/⅔ cup milk
oil, for greasing

1 Preheat the oven to 180°C/350°F/ Gas 4. Sift the flour into a bowl with the baking powder. Add a pinch of salt. Rub in the butter with your fingertips to form crumbs. Place the potato flakes in bowl and pour over 200ml/7fl oz/scant 1 cup boiling water. Beat well and cool slightly.

2 Stir the potatoes into the dry ingredients with the herbs and milk.

3 Bring the mixture together to form a soft dough. Turn out on to a floured surface and knead the dough very gently for a few minutes, until soft and pliable.

COOK'S TIP
Don't be tempted to overseason the mixture, as once cooked the baking powder can also increase the salty flavour of the finished scone and this can overpower the taste of the herbs.

4 Roll the dough out on a floured surface to about 4cm/1½in thickness and stamp out rounds using a 7.5cm/3in cutter. Reshape any remaining dough and re-roll for more scones. Place the scones on to a greased baking dish and brush the surfaces with a little more milk.

5 Cook for 15–20 minutes and serve warm. They can be eaten plain, or with a filling.

GRATED CHEESE AND ONION POTATO BREAD

A PLAITED LOAF WITH A CRISP CHEESE AND ONION TOPPING. IDEALLY YOU SHOULD SERVE THIS BREAD BY PULLING CHUNKS OFF THE LOAF RATHER THAN SLICING, SO THAT YOU GET MASSES OF TOPPING WITH EACH BITE. THIS BREAD IS PARTICULARLY DELICIOUS SERVED WARM.

MAKES A 900G/2LB LOAF

INGREDIENTS
    225g/8oz floury potatoes
    350g/12oz/3 cups strong white flour
    7.5ml/1½ tsp easy-blend dried yeast
    25g/1oz/2 tbsp butter, diced
    50g/2oz/½ cup pitted green or
      black olives
For the topping
    30ml/2 tbsp olive oil
    1 onion, sliced into rings
    50g/2oz/½ cup mature Cheddar
      cheese, grated
    salt and ground black pepper

1 Chop the potatoes and cook in a large saucepan with plenty of salted boiling water for 15–20 minutes or until tender.

2 Meanwhile, sift the flour into a bowl, add the yeast and a little salt. Rub in the butter to form fine crumbs. Drain the potatoes and mash well. Add to the dry ingredients with 300ml/½ pint/1¼ cups lukewarm water.

3 Bring the mixture together with a round-bladed knife and then turn out on to a floured surface. Knead for about 5 minutes. Return the dough to a bowl and cover with a damp cloth. Leave to rise for 1 hour or until doubled in size. Turn the dough out onto a floured surface and knock back to remove any air bubbles. Carefully knead in the olives. Cut the dough into three even pieces.

4 Roll each piece out to a long thick sausage. Twist the sausages over each other to form a plait (see Cook's Tip, below). Lift on to a greased baking sheet. Cover with a damp cloth and leave to rise for 30 minutes or until doubled in size.

COOK'S TIP
To plait a loaf successfully, lay the three lengths of dough side by side. Plait the dough from one end to the centre and repeat with the other end. This will give an even loaf with a professional looking touch to it.

5 Meanwhile, for the topping, preheat the oven to 220°C/425°F/Gas 7. Heat the oil in a saucepan and fry the onions for 10 minutes until golden.

6 Remove the onions from the pan and drain on kitchen paper.

7 Scatter the onions and grated cheese over the bread and bake in the oven for 20 minutes.

RUSSIAN POTATO BREAD

POTATOES ARE PART OF THE STAPLE DIET IN RUSSIA AND ARE OFTEN USED TO REPLACE SOME OF THE FLOUR IN BREAD RECIPES. THE RESULT IS A LOVELY, MOIST LOAF WHICH IS DELICIOUS JUST SERVED WITH BUTTER. THIS EASY-TO-MAKE BREAD ALSO KEEPS REALLY WELL.

MAKES ONE LOAF

INGREDIENTS
  butter, for greasing
  225g/8oz floury potatoes, diced
  6g/¼oz sachet easy-blend
    dried yeast
  350g/12oz/3 cups unbleached white
    bread flour
  115g/4oz/1 cup wholemeal
    bread flour, plus extra for sprinkling
  2.5ml/½ tsp caraway seeds, crushed
  10ml/2 tsp salt
  25g/1oz/2 tbsp butter, diced

1 Lightly grease a baking sheet. Cook the potatoes in boiling water until tender. Drain well, reserving 150ml/ ¼ pint/⅔ cup of the cooking water. Mash and sieve the potatoes and leave to cool.

2 Mix together the yeast, white bread flour, wholemeal bread flour, caraway seeds and salt in a large bowl. Add the butter, cut into small pieces and rub in to form a breadcrumb consistency.

3 Mix together the reserved potato water and sieved potatoes. Gradually work this mixture into the flour mixture to form a soft dough.

4 Turn out on to a lightly floured surface and knead for 8–10 minutes until smooth and elastic.

5 Place the dough in a large, lightly oiled bowl, cover with lightly oiled clear film and leave to rise, in a warm place, for about 1 hour, or until it has doubled in size.

VARIATION
Omit the caraway seeds and knead 115g/4oz/1 cup grated or crumbled Cheddar, Red Leicester or blue cheese into the dough before shaping.

6 Turn out on to a lightly floured surface, knock back and knead gently. Shape into a plump oval loaf about 18cm/7in long. Place on the prepared baking sheet and sprinkle with a little wholemeal bread flour.

7 Cover with lightly oiled clear film and leave to rise, in a warm place, for 30 minutes, or until doubled in size.

8 Meanwhile preheat the oven to 200°C/400°F/Gas 6. Using a sharp knife, slash the top with 3–4 diagonal cuts to make a criss-cross effect.

9 Bake for 30–35 minutes until golden and hollow sounding when tapped on the base. Transfer to a wire rack to cool.

KARTOFFELBROT

THIS IS AN ADAPTATION OF THE CLASSIC GERMAN-STYLE BREAD, THIS VERSION IS MADE WITH
STRONG WHITE FLOUR AND FLOURY POTATOES.

MAKES A 450G/1LB LOAF

INGREDIENTS
    butter, for greasing
    225g/8oz/2 cups strong white flour
    10ml/2 tsp baking powder
    5ml/1 tsp salt
    175g/6oz potatoes, cooked
     and mashed
    15ml/1 tbsp vegetable oil
    paprika, for dusting
    mustard-flavoured butter, to serve

COOK'S TIP
This bread is best eaten warm with
lashings of mustard-flavoured butter.

1 Preheat the oven to 230°C/450°F/
Gas 8. Grease and line a 450g/1lb loaf tin.

2 Sift the flour into a large bowl and
mix together with baking powder and
the salt.

3 Rub the mashed potato into the dry
ingredients making sure you achieve an
even mixture.

4 Stir in the oil and 200ml/7fl oz/scant
1 cup lukewarm water. Turn the dough
into the tin and dust with the paprika.
Bake in the oven for 25 minutes. Turn
out on to a wire rack to cool. Cut the
bread into thick chunks and serve with
mustard-flavoured butter.

SAVOURY CRANBERRY AND POTATO BREAD SLICE

AN INTERESTING COMBINATION OF CRANBERRIES WITH BACON AND POTATOES. THE CRANBERRIES COLOUR THE BREAD SLICES, GIVING IT A VERY FESTIVE FEEL.

MAKES A 450G/1LB LOAF

INGREDIENTS
450g/1lb/4 cups strong white flour
5ml/1 tsp easy-blend dried yeast
5ml/1 tsp salt
25g/1oz/2 tbsp butter, diced
325ml/11fl oz/1⅓ cups
  lukewarm water
75g/3oz/¾ cup fresh or frozen
  cranberries, thawed
oil, for greasing
225g/8oz floury potatoes, halved
6 rashers rindless streaky
  bacon, chopped
30ml/2 tbsp runny honey
salt and ground black pepper

1 Sift the flour into a bowl, stir in the yeast and 5ml/1 tsp salt. Rub in the butter to form breadcrumbs. Make a well in the centre and stir in the water.

2 Bring the mixture together with a round-bladed knife and then turn out on to a floured surface. Knead for 5 minutes. Place the dough in a bowl and cover with a damp cloth. Leave to rise for 1 hour or until doubled in size.

COOK'S TIP
If you can't find fresh or frozen cranberries, substitute them with sweetcorn niblets.

3 Turn the dough out and knock back to remove the air bubbles. Knead for a few minutes. Carefully knead the cranberries into the bread. Roll the dough out to a rectangle and place in an oiled 23 x 23cm/9 x 9in flan tin. Push the dough into the corners and cover with a damp cloth. Leave to rise in a warm place for 30 minutes.

4 Preheat the oven to 220°C/425°F/ Gas 7. Meanwhile, boil the potatoes in plenty of salted water for 15 minutes or until just tender. Drain and when cool enough to handle, slice thinly.

5 Scatter the potatoes and bacon over the risen bread dough, season, then drizzle with the honey and bake for 25 minutes, covering the bread loosely with foil after 20 minutes to prevent burning.

6 Remove the bread from the oven and transfer to a wire rack. Return to the oven for 5 minutes to crisp the base. Leave to cool on the wire rack.

DILL AND POTATO SCONES

POTATO SCONES FLAVOURED WITH DILL ARE QUITE SCRUMPTIOUS AND CAN BE SERVED WARM JUST WITH BUTTER. OR IF YOU WANT TO MAKE THEM SUBSTANTIAL ENOUGH FOR A LIGHT SUPPER, SERVE THEM TOPPED WITH FLAKED SALMON, KIPPER OR MACKEREL.

MAKES ABOUT TEN

INGREDIENTS
  oil, for greasing
  225g/8oz/2 cups self-raising flour
  40g/1½oz/3 tbsp butter, softened
  pinch of salt
  15ml/1 tbsp finely chopped fresh dill
  175g/6oz mashed potato,
    freshly made
  30–45ml/2–3 tbsp milk

COOK'S TIP
If you don't have any dill you can replace it with the herb of your choice. Try fresh parsley or basil as an alternative.

1 Preheat the oven to 230°C/450°F/ Gas 8. Grease a baking sheet. Sift the flour into a bowl, and rub in the butter with your fingertips. Add the salt and dill and stir.

2 Add the mashed potato to the mixture and enough milk to make a soft, pliable dough.

3 Turn out the dough on to a well-floured surface and roll out until it is fairly thin. Cut into rounds using a 7.5cm/3in cutter.

4 Place the scones on the prepared baking sheet, leaving space between each one, and bake for 20–25 minutes until risen and golden. Serve warm.

SAVOURY POTATO DROP SCONES

A LIGHT SCONE WITH A MILD MUSTARD AND CHEESE FLAVOUR, THESE MAKE A DELICIOUS BREAKFAST DISH SERVED WITH SCRAMBLED EGGS AND GRILLED TOMATOES.

MAKES SIXTEEN

INGREDIENTS
  175g/6oz floury potatoes, diced
  115g/4oz/1 cup self-raising flour
  5ml/1 tsp mustard powder
  1 egg, beaten
  25g/1oz/¼ cup Cheddar cheese,
    grated
  150ml/¼ pint/⅔ cup milk
  oil, for frying and greasing
  salt and freshly ground black pepper
  butter, to serve

COOK'S TIP
It is best to use a flat griddle rather than a ridged one for this recipe as the scones are quite small and thin.

1 Cook the potatoes in plenty of boiling salted water for 20 minutes or until tender. Drain the potatoes and then mash them well.

2 Spoon the mashed potato from the saucepan into a large mixing bowl and then add the flour, mustard powder, egg, cheese and milk.

3 Beat well until the mixture comes together. Season.

4 Heat a griddle pan and brush with oil. Drop tablespoonfuls of the mixture on to the griddle and cook for 1–2 minutes. Flip the scones over and cook the second side. Repeat to make 16 scones. Serve warm with butter.

CHOCOLATE POTATO CAKE

THIS IS A VERY RICH, MOIST CHOCOLATE CAKE, TOPPED WITH A THIN LAYER OF CHOCOLATE ICING.
USE A GOOD-QUALITY DARK CHOCOLATE FOR BEST RESULTS AND SERVE WITH WHIPPED CREAM.

MAKES A 23CM/9IN CAKE

INGREDIENTS
    oil, for greasing
    200g/7oz/1 cup sugar
    250g/9oz/1 cup and 2 tbsp butter
    4 eggs, separated
    275g/10oz dark chocolate
    75g/3oz/¾ cup ground almonds
    165g/5½oz mashed potato
    225g/8oz/2 cups self-raising flour
    5ml/1 tsp cinnamon
    45ml/3 tbsp milk
    white and dark chocolate shavings,
      to garnish
    whipped cream, to serve

1 Preheat the oven to 180°C/350°F/
Gas 4. Grease and base-line a
23cm/9in round cake tin with a circle of
baking parchment.

2 In a large bowl, cream together
the sugar and 225g/8oz/1 cup of the
butter until light and fluffy. Then beat
the egg yolks into the creamed
mixture one at a time until it is smooth
and creamy.

3 Finely chop or grate 175g/6oz of the
chocolate and stir it into the creamed
mixture with the ground almonds. Pass
the mashed potato through a sieve or
ricer and stir it into the creamed
chocolate mixture.

4 Sift together the flour and cinnamon
and fold into the mixture with the milk.

COOK'S TIP
Chocolate can be melted very
successfully in the microwave. Place
the pieces of chocolate in a plastic
measuring jug or bowl. The chocolate
may scorch if placed in a glass bowl.
Microwave on high for 1 minute, stir,
and then heat again for up to
1 minute, checking halfway through
to see if it is done.

5 Whisk the egg whites until they hold
stiff but not dry peaks, and fold into the
cake mixture.

6 Spoon into the prepared tin and
smooth over the top, but make a slight
hollow in the middle to help keep the
surface of the cake level during
cooking. Bake in the oven for 1¼ hours
until a wooden toothpick inserted in the
centre comes out clean. Allow the cake
to cool slightly in the tin, then turn out
and cool on a wire rack.

7 Meanwhile break up the remaining
chocolate into a heatproof bowl and
stand it over a saucepan of hot water.
Add the remaining butter in small
pieces and stir well until the chocolate
has melted and the mixture is smooth
and glossy.

8 Peel off the lining paper and trim
the top of the cake so that it is level.
Smooth over the chocolate icing and
allow to set. Decorate with white and
dark chocolate shavings and serve with
lashings of whipped cream.

INDEX

ACKNOWLEDGEMENTS

Of the many people and organizations who have patiently answered my persistent questioning by phone, fax or email, Alex Barker and the publishers would like to thank the following:
Three Countries Potatoes, (David Chappel of Newport, Norman Hosking of Penzance, Morrice Innes of Aberdeenshire and Andrew McQueen of Shrewsbury) – especially for providing so many potato samples for photography; Alan Wilson (Agronomist and Potato Specialist to Waitrose) and The Story of the Potato by Alan Wilson published by Alan Wilson; Alan Romans – and his Guide to Seed Potato Varieties published by the Henry Doubleday Research Organisation, Ryton Organic Gardens, Coventry CV8 3LG UK; David Turnbull and Stuart Carnegie at the Scottish Agricultural Science Agency; Nicola Bark of Vegfed, Huddart Parker Building, Post Office Square, PO Box 10232, Wellington, New Zealand Tel 644472 3795 Fax 644471 2861 www.vegfed.co.nz; Lori Wing,

The Potato Association of America, University of Maine, 5715 Coburn Hall, #6 Orono, ME 04469 5715; Kathleen Haynes @asrr.arsusda.gov; Dr Alvin Reeves REEVES@ MAINE.MAINE.EDU; Carl Duivenvoorden, New Brunswick Agriexport Inc., 850 Lincoln Rd PO Box 1101, Station "A", Fredericton, New Brunswick, Canada E3B 5C2 Tel 506 453 2890 Fax 506 453 7170; Peter Boswall, Prince Edward Island Agriculture & Forestry, PO Box 1600, Charlottetown, Prince Edward Island, Canada CIA 7N3 Tel 902 368 5600 Fax 902 368 5729; An Bord Glas, 8-11 Lower Baggot Street, Dublin 2; Dr F Ezeta and Christine Graves, The International Potato Centre, Lima, Peru; The British Potato Council, 4300 Nash Court, John Smith Drive, Oxford Business Park, South, Oxford OX4 2RT; Phil Harlock at Covent Garden Supply Co., A24-29 New Covent Garden Market, London SW8 5LR; Colin Randel, Mr Fothergill's Seeds, Kentford, Newmarket, Suffolk CB8 7QB Tel 01638 751 161 Fax 01638 751 624. Not forgetting the

many other companies, farmers, producers and experts worldwide who have helped answer my numerous questions.

For potato samples for photography:
Glens of Antrim Potatoes, Red Bay, Cushendall, Co Antrim, BT44 0SH; ASDA; J Sainsbury plc; Waitrose

For the generous loan of photographic props:
David Mellor, 4 Sloane Square, London SW1
Tel 020 7730 4259
Divertimenti, 139-141 Fulham Rd, London SW3 6SD
Mail Order 020 8246 4300
Elizabeth David Cookshop, Covent Garden, London WC2
Tel 020 7836 9167
Kenwood Ltd, New Lane, Havant, Hampshire PO9 2NH
Tel 023 9247 6000
Magimix UK Ltd, 115A High Street, Godalming, Surrey GU7 1AQ Tel 01483 427 411

Thank you to Stephanie England for her styling, hand modelling and days of telephone research.

Useful reference publications:
The Netherlands Catalogue of Potato Varieties 1997, published by NIVAA.
The Potato Variety Handbook published by NIAB (The National Institute of Agricultural Botany) Huntingdon Rd, Cambridge CB3 OLE UK.
Potato Varieties in Canada 1997, produced by the New Brunswick Department of Agriculture, Canada.
Classification of Potato Varieties in the Reference Collection at East Craigs, Edinburgh, by Douglas M Macdonald, published by the Scottish Office Agriculture and Fisheries Department.
Atlantic Canada Potato Guide published by authority of the Atlantic Provinces Agriculture Services Co-ordinating Committee, New Brunswick, Canada.
EC Common Catalogue Vol 40, (Plant Varieties and Seeds Gazette) from The Stationery Office Ltd, 51 Nine Elms, London SW8 4DR.
North American Potato Varieties Handbooks published by the Potato Association of America.

NOTES

Notes

NOTES

NOTES